SYMPOSIUM

PLATO

Symposium

Translated,
with Introduction
& Notes, by

ALEXANDER NEHAMAS

&

PAUL WOODRUFF

Hackett Publishing Company
Indianapolis & Cambridge

Plato: ca. 428–347 B.C.

For further information, please
address the publisher:

Hackett Publishing Company
P.O. Box 44937
Indianapolis, Indiana 46244-0937

Cover illustration:
Cover of a mirror,
second half of fifth century B.C.
New York, Metropolitan Museum

Interior design by Dan Kirklin

Library of Congress Cataloging-in-Publication Data

Plato
[Symposium. English]
Symposium/Plato: translated, with introduction & notes, by
Alexander Nehamas & Paul Woodruff.
p.   cm.
Bibliography: p.
ISBN 0-87220-077-9—ISBN 0-87220-076-0 (pbk.)
1. Socrates.
2. Love—Early works to 1800.
I. Nehamas, Alexander, 1946–
II. Woodruff, Paul, 1943–
III. Title.
B385.A5N44   1989
184—dc19   89-30960
CIP

The paper used in this publication
meets the minimum requirements of
the American National Standard for Information Sciences—
Permanence of Paper for Printed Library Materials,
ANSI Z39.48 1984.

CONTENTS

Note to the Reader   ix
Introduction   xi
Note on the Translation   xxvii

Introductory Dialogue   1
The Speech of Phaedrus   9
The Speech of Pausanias   13
The Speech of Eryximachus   20
The Speech of Aristophanes   25
The Speech of Agathon   32
Socrates Questions Agathon   40
Diotima Questions Socrates   45
The Speech of Diotima   48
Alcibiades' Entrance   61
The Speech of Alcibiades   65
Final Dialogue   76

Selected Bibliography   79

This Book Is Dedicated
to the Memory of
WILLIAM H. Y. HACKETT
(1921–1986)

NOTE TO
THE READER

This translation is as nearly as possible a joint product. Alexander Nehamas wrote the introduction, and Paul Woodruff wrote the notes. We are grateful to the late William Hackett, whose idea it was for us to do this, and to John Cooper, whose pencil has improved virtually every page.

INTRODUCTION

THE *SYMPOSIUM* is one of Plato's best known and most influential works. Its importance and its popularity derive from a number of factors which are as exhilarating in themselves as they are difficult to put together into a unified whole. The dialogue presents at least four different aspects to its readers, and it is read for at least four different reasons. First of all, the *Symposium* contains a series of speeches on the subject of love (*erōs*), and this is the main reason most readers are attracted to it. Second, it contains one of the most explicit and vivid descriptions of a Platonic "Form," the Form of Beauty, which, according to Socrates' speech, is the final object of all love (209E–212A); the dialogue accordingly provides crucial information on the nature of those objects which Plato considered as the ultimate constituents of reality. Third, the *Symposium* provides an extraordinary portrait of Socrates, through his own words, through the comments of the other participants in the feast which is the dialogue's subject, and through the long speech of Alcibiades (215A–222B). Finally, on a more formal level, the *Symposium* is one of the most artfully dramatic works of philosophy ever composed. Plato's success in presenting abstract philosophical ideas of an otherworldly sort through a lighthearted, often comic piece of writing is in itself an object of admiration and study.

The *Symposium* is an account of a banquet given by the young poet Agathon to celebrate his first victory (with his first play, no less) at the dramatic contest held in conjunction with the Lenaian Festival in Athens in 416 B.C. Socrates, who would have been over fifty at that time, is by far the oldest member of the company. The account of the banquet is given by a certain Apollodorus, sometime between 406 and 400 B.C., as we can gather from his statement that, at the time he is asked to relate what occurred at the feast, Agathon has been absent from Athens "for many years" (172C). As for the actual dialogue, two allusions to historical events (182B, 193A) show that Plato must have written

it after 385 B.C.,[1] while the fact that Phaedrus speaks only hypo-
thetically of a regiment composed of lovers (178E−179B) implies
that it was completed before 378 B.C., when the city of Thebes
established just such a regiment, the famous "Sacred Band."

We have no positive evidence that the dinner Plato describes
actually ever took place. On the other hand, nothing excludes
the possibility, even though the historical Aristophanes, who is
on very good terms with everyone here, had already attacked
Socrates in his play *The Clouds* and would soon turn against
Agathon in his *Thesmophoriazousai*. Nevertheless, Plato goes out
of his way to suggest that Apollodorus, the dialogue's narrator, is
only repeating an account he has heard from someone else
(173B). Since Plato uses such an indirect approach in the *Parmenides*, a dialogue relating a conversation which could not have
taken place, we may speculate that at least the details of the
occasion the *Symposium* describes, if not the occasion itself, are
Plato's own invention.

This speculation is made more plausible when we consider
the fact that the crucial part of Socrates' speech on *erōs* is supposed to be an account of the views of Diotima, a priestess from
Mantineia, of whom we know nothing other than what Socrates
tells us here. In addition, Diotima in her speech makes an allusion to the view Aristophanes has just presented at the banquet
(204D−E, 212C). This, too, suggests that even if Diotima actually
existed, what she is represented as saying to Socrates cannot
have been composed, as Socrates claims, long before the party
during which he relates it. Furthermore, Plato's having Socrates
admit that he cannot understand Diotima (206B) and having Diotima warn him that he may not be capable of being initiated
into "the final and highest mystery" of love (210A) may well be

---

1. It is remotely possible that, in 193A, Aristophanes may be referring to
an earlier division of the Mantineian Alliance on the part of the Spartans in 418 B.C. (cf. Thucydides V.81). But the word Aristophanes uses
here is not strictly appropriate to that action, and, in any case, the
allusion at 182B (to the subjection of Ionia, on the coast of Asia Minor, to
the Persian Empire, which occurred in 386 B.C.) is sufficient to fix the
date of the dialogue.

Plato's way of indicating that the views involved toward the end
of Socrates' speech are not Socrates' but Plato's own.[2]

"Dinner party" or even "feast" is not a perfect translation of
the Greek word *symposion*, which literally means "drinking together." Though food was always served on such occasions, it
was consumed quickly at the start of the evening so that the
participants could get to the real purpose of the affair. This was
heavy drinking, usually under the direction of an elected
"leader" (*symposiarchos*), who had the authority to propose end-
less toasts, usually drunk in order from left to right, and to
establish how much each guest would have to consume. Enter-
tainment, both musical and sexual, was commonly supplied by
flute-girls (*aulētrides*), and the evenings would often end with
the guests dropping off to an exhausted sleep on the couches
on which they had been eating and drinking throughout the
evening.

The guests at Agathon's dinner, however, are suffering the
aftereffects of the previous night's drinking, and they decide
early on to drink lightly and to send the flute-girl away
(176A–E). Instead, they decide to have a conversation on—or,
rather, a series of speeches in praise of—*erōs* (176E–177E). Such
speeches, too, are given in order from left to right, making
Socrates, who comes to the dinner late and shares Agathon's
couch, the last to take the floor.

The general Greek word for "love" is *philia*, which applies
indifferently to the feelings of friends, family members, and
lovers. *Erōs* refers to particularly intense attachment and desire
in general. Most commonly, however, it is applied to passionate
love and desire, usually sexual, and to the god who personified
that state. Since Greek lacked our convention of capitalizing the

---

2. A number of the views Socrates expresses in the first part of his dialogue with Diotima are views compatible with other views expressed
in Plato's Socratic dialogues. But the idea that love is the desire for
"birth in (the presence of) beauty" (206c ff.) and everything that follows,
including, of course, the revelation of the Form of Beauty as the ultimate object of *erōs* (209E–212A) is Plato's; cf. Vlastos, "The Individual as
Object of Love in Plato," p. 21, n. 58.

initials of proper names, it is only possible to tell what the word refers to in each case from the context, and our translation constantly shifts between "he" (to refer to the god) and "it" (to refer to the state). *Erōs* and *philia* can coexist; this becomes obvious in Phaedrus' discussion of the example of Alcestis, who alone was willing to die in her husband's place: "Because of her love (*erōs*), she went so far beyond his parents in family feeling (*philia*) that she made them look like outsiders" (179C).

But despite the case of Alcestis, which is also mentioned (though with a vastly different interpretation) by Diotima (208D), the love discussed and praised in the *Symposium* is primarily homosexual. It is true that Eryximachus in his speech generalizes the phenomenon to apply to almost everything in the world and that Aristophanes places homosexual and heterosexual love on exactly the same footing. But Pausanias and Agathon are totally unconcerned with heterosexuality; Phaedrus mentions it almost as an afterthought; and Socrates places it, along with the desire to procreate, outside the "ladder of love" which leads from the love of one particular beautiful boy to the love of Beauty itself.

Plato's emphasis on homosexual love is not always easy for his twentieth-century audience to understand. It is, actually, a remarkable fact that the *Symposium*, the first explicit discussion of love in western literature and philosophy, begins as a discussion of homosexual love and soon leaves behind all love of individuals: the real objects of love, as the concluding parts of Socrates' speech (208C–212A) urge, are fame, beautiful bodies in general, beautiful souls, the beauty in laws, practices, and the sciences, and finally Beauty itself, in all its purity and generality.

In fact, these two features of the *Symposium*—that the love addressed is primarily homosexual and that it soon becomes very abstract and general indeed—are interconnected. Greek homosexual relations often had a crucial educational and ethical dimension, which Plato took over and developed in the abstract direction dictated by his theoretical philosophical views.

In ancient Athens, it was both accepted and expected that older men would fall in love with and seek sexual gratification from younger (that is, adolescent) boys. Such relationships generally existed side by side with conventional marriage on the part of the older man, the "lover" (*erastēs*), and with the expectation of it on the part of the boy, the "beloved" (erōmenos). The affairs were asymmetrical in a number of ways. For one thing, the boy was supposed to be won only with difficulty and to resist the passionate and often extravagant advances of the lover. Second, once won, the beloved was expected not to enjoy the sexual act; on the contrary, enjoyment was a sign of a depraved nature. As Xenophon wrote in his own Symposium (viii.21), "The boy does not share in the man's pleasure in intercourse, as a woman does; cold sober, he looks upon the other drunk with sexual desire."[3] Finally, the relationship, at least ideally, involved the lover in the role of ethical and intellectual teacher and the boy in the role of his student. The latter had everything to learn from and nothing to teach the former; in fact, a proper homosexual relationship was often a crucial part of the socialization of the sons of good families into adult civic life. Once the boy reached adulthood, he ceased being a beloved and became a friend: the affair was over. Long-lasting relationships between adults, like that between Agathon and Pausanias (cf. 193B–C), were the exception rather than the rule. Actually, Athenian attitudes toward homosexual affairs were not entirely consistent. Young boys were protected by their families from the advances of older men, who were nevertheless urged to pursue them and were admired for their conquests. Despite the ethical benefits of such relationships, giving in to a lover, especially too quickly, was often considered a disgrace.

The praises of erōs in the Symposium can be roughly divided into two groups. The first three speeches, by Phaedrus, Pausanias, and Eryximachus, naturally fall into one category, and the second three, by Aristophanes, Agathon, and Socrates, into another.

The first group of speeches is rather conventional in its praise of erōs for its effects, though all three speakers seem to be trying to come to terms with the double standard implicit in the attitudes of Athens toward pederasty and to defend erōs against charges that must have been commonplace at the time.

None of these speeches, however, is purely conventional. Phaedrus' passionate emphasis on virtue and self-sacrifice, for

---

3. Quoted in K.J. Dover, Greek Homosexuality, p. 52. This study is indispensable for an understanding of Greek, especially Athenian, attitudes.

example, goes beyond common practice. His style is simple, but carefully balanced and concise. His enthusiasm, however, carries him to say extravagant things: that love is the best guide to virtue (a view also shared by Socrates, but on the basis of a radically different conception of *erōs*) and that virtue is most valuable when connected with love. The virtue that interests him is the courage that leads to self-sacrifice, and in developing that theme he twists the legend of Orpheus to suit his purposes (179D). Love has no dark side in Phaedrus' eyes, and his praise of its effects is indiscriminate.

Pausanias is unwilling to share Phaedrus' unlimited enthusiasm. He continues to praise *erōs's* effects but distinguishes between a vulgar and a noble kind of love. The former, he argues, is aimed indifferently at women as well as at boys: its purpose is purely sexual gratification. The latter, which is exclusively homosexual, is concerned with the welfare of the beloved's soul. There is something self-serving and self-righteous in Pausanias' rather prim attitude. And it is not at all impossible that Aristophanes, who developed the hiccups while Pausanias is talking (185C−E), may have exploited his problem to make fun of Pausanias. In any case, it is worth bearing in mind that Aristophanes is hiccupping during at least part of Pausanias' high-minded oration.

Pausanias' distinction between noble and vulgar love is taken over by Eryximachus, who stretches the meaning of "love" into "attraction" or even "harmony." This, in turn, enables him to credit love, without defining it any further, with beneficial effects not only in medicine (which, he never tires of reminding us, is his own field) but also in music, meteorology, and divination. Eryximachus' style, like his manner throughout the *Symposium*, is extremely pedantic. Plato is clearly satirizing his self-importance and his extraordinarily good opinion of the significance of medicine. In general, it is remarkable how many of the speeches in this work contain elements of parody: even Socrates' habit of engaging in dialectic through the method of question and answer does not escape unscathed (194A−E, 199B ff.).

Aristophanes' magnificent speech, with which the second group of speeches begins, is in sharp contrast to Eryximachus' vague abstractions, bringing the discussion back to the subject of the feelings of individual people for one another. Aristophanes

tells a myth according to which human beings were originally of
three sexes—male, female, and male-female—and had twice as
many limbs and organs as we have today. For a number of reasons, the gods decided to split them in half, and accordingly
each one of us today is searching for a half of the same original
nature with whom to spend the rest of our life. Love is the desire
to find our other original half, and our sexual preference is de-
termined by the sex of the original double being from which
each of us is descended. Aristophanes' story thus interprets both
homosexual and heterosexual love as absolutely natural, but it
makes another crucial contribution to the speeches' progression.

Aristophanes' speech is stunning in its originality. Although
it contains parody in its use of myth, it is on the whole a highly
serious work, and its view of love has no parallel in earlier Greek
literature. It actually anticipates more romantic modern versions
of love, particularly the idea that love draws together two unique
individuals to join as one person. For all its comic elements, a
sad note sounds frequently in the speech: the goal of loving, the
forging of one person out of two, is not to be achieved. What we
have instead is the temporary satisfaction of sexual relationships, and these are at best a promise of a more permanent
happiness and a closer union.

By giving an explanation, however fanciful, of the desire people have to spend large parts of their life in the company of
someone else, Aristophanes shifts attention from the benefits of
love to its nature—something the first group of speeches either
neglected or underemphasized. And this is precisely the strategy
Agathon adopts in his own encomium: "You must explain what
qualities in the subject of your speech enable him to give the
benefits for which we praise him," he says at the very beginning
of his contribution (195A). He then proceeds, in a masterful parody of oratory, to praise *erōs* as the youngest, the most beautiful,
and the most virtuous of the gods and to account for Love's
benefits by relating them directly to his youth, beauty, and
virtue.

This is, delightfully, the most comic of these six speeches.
And though Agathon is a tragedian, Socrates will later contend
that a good tragic poet should also be able to write in comic vein
(223D). No doubt Plato means us to notice that neither his tragic
nor his comic poet—Aristophanes—follows exclusively his own

special muse. Here, the young speaker, quite drunk already in
his own honor, is unmistakably playing for laughs. He indulges
in an unrestrained parody of Gorgianic style and sophistic argument, enlivened with salacious double entendres, and punctu-
ated with digs at the age and ugliness of his couch partner,
Socrates. Still, as he himself insists, though much of the speech
is mock-serious, parts of it are meant in earnest.

Socrates has nothing but praise for Agathon's method of
speaking first of the features of *erōs* and only then of its benefits,
which fits well with his own dialectical practice (cf. *Meno* 71B).
But he accepts none of the conclusions Agathon has reached
through that method. In characteristic manner, which does
however seem a little out of place on such an occasion, he questions Agathon in the manner in which he usually questions
his interlocutors in Plato's more explicitly dialectical works
(199C–201C). He gets Agathon to agree that *erōs* is the desire for
beauty (a first attempt at a definition of its nature). He then
claims that, since no one desires what one already has or is, *erōs*
cannot be beautiful. For that matter, in view of the fact that all
good things are beautiful, *erōs* cannot be good or virtuous either
(199C–201C).

Having silenced Agathon, Socrates now tactfully tells him
that he himself had made the mistake of thinking that *erōs* was
beautiful and good at one point in life. He was corrected by
Diotima, a priestess from the city of Mantineia, who was his
teacher in all matters of love, and he now goes on to relate his
conversation with her. The upshot of this conversation is that
erōs turns out to be neither beautiful nor ugly but something "in
between"; and the same is true for his goodness, his divinity,
and his wisdom: "he is in love with what is beautiful, and
wisdom is extremely beautiful. It follows that Love *must* be a
lover of wisdom (*philosophos*/philosopher), and, as such, is in
between being wise and being ignorant" (204B).

The reason Agathon and the younger Socrates were tempted
to attribute all good qualities to *erōs* turns out to be that they
conceived of it on the model of the beloved, who is the object of
desire and is thus young, beautiful, and good and not—as would
have been correct—on the model of the lover, who lacks these
features but is still close enough to them to recognize and appre-
ciate them (204C). We must keep this idea in mind, for it will

become important when we turn to the *Symposium's* portrait of Socrates. But the point is also important in the immediate context, because it shows that Plato has already begun to mould the conventional conception of love to suit his own philosophical needs. We have seen that the lover was traditionally expected to be his beloved's teacher: wisdom, that is, was the lover's contribution to a relationship in which the beloved supplied only physical beauty. But by counting wisdom among beautiful things, Socrates has turned the lover from a purveyor into a pursuer of wisdom. This, in a way, is one of the most crucial ideas presented in the *Symposium*, and it governs all that follows in Socrates' speech: philosophy, the pursuit of wisdom, is motivated by love; it is, in fact, love's highest expression.

Diotima defines *erōs* in general as the desire for the continual possession of good things (206A). But since this is equivalent to defining it as the desire for happiness (204E), she tries to offer a more specific account which will apply to love and sexual desire in particular. She goes on to say that love specifically is the desire to reproduce and to "give birth in beauty" (206B, E). "All of us," she claims, "are pregnant . . . both in body and in soul, and as soon as we come to a certain age, we naturally desire to give birth" (206C).[4] This desire to reproduce, which is also a desire for immortality (206E–207A), may involve physical offspring, glory, or good deeds in general—anything that springs from the individual but stays behind after the individual's death.

For Plato, and so for Socrates and Diotima in the *Symposium*, the most lasting offspring are virtuous acts. These are produced by a lover who is attracted by a noble soul within a boy's beautiful body (lovers who are only pregnant "in their body" are attracted to women, according to Diotima) and who, together with his beloved, leaves behind him "more beautiful and more immortal" children (209C). Such, for example, are "the children" of the great poets and the great lawmakers of Greece (209D).

Socrates' speech could well have ended at this point. To be sure, there are serious differences between it and the speeches that preceded it. It begins, for example, with a dialectical bout

---

4. On this strange reversal, which makes the pregnancy the cause and not the outcome of intercourse, see M.F. Burnyeat, "Socratic Midwifery, Platonic Inspiration."

which is, to say the least, unusual in the context of a formal encomium. Socrates' attribution of the views he presents to Diotima and his recounting of his imaginary conversation with her are unprecedented in the history of rhetoric. The idea that *erōs* is "a philosopher" and the definition of love as the desire to give "birth in beauty" are clear innovations on Plato's part, and the tone of the speech, despite some light touches here and there, is much more serious than that of any of the others, rising to a remarkable crescendo at 208C−209E. Despite all these differences, however, Socrates' speech has, up to this point, been quite continuous with all the others. Socrates has concentrated on the love of individuals for one another and, despite his various disagreements with the earlier speakers, has attributed to this love the same general sort of benefits which Phaedrus and Pausanias had introduced into the discussion. His speech is more complex than any other, but it has not so far added anything truly novel to the picture of *erōs*.

It is just here, however, at the point where Plato's readers, familiar with the conventions of formal speeches of praise (*encōmia*), would have been ready for Socrates to stop, that something remarkable occurs. Instead of winding his speech down, Socrates reports that Diotima told him that everything she had said about love up to this point, far from exhausting the topic (as it would have been perfectly natural to suppose), constituted only the means and stepping-stones for something else, "the final and highest mystery" of love. And she tells him that, though she will try to explain that mystery to him, he may well be unable to understand it (210A).

Now we are on completely new ground. Diotima describes a kind of "ascent" of love (210A−210D). A lover first falls in love with a single beautiful body, which inspires him to give birth to beautiful ideas. But the lover, as we know, loves beauty, and the beauty in all beautiful bodies is the same: the lover, therefore, will realize that his reasons for loving a single individual are also reasons for his becoming a lover of all beautiful bodies, and he values his earlier love less than before. The lover now sees that the beauty of the soul is nobler than the beauty of bodies, and he turns to the creation of "such ideas as will make young men better." In looking for such "ideas" or "discourses" (*logoi*), the lover will come to realize that the "activities and laws" which such ideas express are themselves beautiful in their own right and will devote himself to them instead. But these activities and laws, in turn, manifest and depend upon knowledge, and the lover now becomes attached to nothing less than "the great sea of beauty, and, gazing upon this, he gives birth to many gloriously beautiful ideas and theories, in unstinting love of wisdom (*philosophia*)."

These are radically new ideas. Plato begins with the ordinary concept of love as a bond uniting two people. He then exploits the view that homosexual affairs had an educational dimension, connects it with his own idea that love is a desire for wisdom, and combines it with what for him is a fundamental assumption, namely, that if we love or desire something for some reason, X, then that reason, X, is the primary object of our love or desire.[5] So at each step of the ascent, the lover "rises" to a love of whatever it is that explains the beauty of, and hence his love for, the object on the step below. Love, then, which by now has almost become another word for philosophy, has left the bonds between individual people far behind: nothing of that sort could have been expected from the first part of Socrates' speech.[6]

But even the love of knowledge, Diotima continues, is not the final stage of this ascent. Emphasizing the novelty and the controversial nature of what we are about to be told (210E), she now reveals "the reason for all [these] earlier labors." If a lover has gone about things correctly, he will at some point "all of a sudden" (*exaiphnēs*: we will return to this) see "the reason for all his earlier labors." This reason, for the sake of which everything else has been undertaken, is Beauty itself, that which makes everything else beautiful and the ultimate object of all *erōs*, according to Plato's highly revisionary and bold view.

This "Form" of Beauty is pure, unchanging, beautiful in every way, not to be seen with the eyes of the body, and separate

---

5. See John A. Brentlinger, "The Nature of Love."
6. Whether love for individuals *as* individuals is completely abandoned or merely receives lesser emphasis is a complex and disputed question. See Gregory Vlastos, "The Individual as Object of Love in Plato," pp. 32–34, for the former view, and T.H. Irwin, *Plato's Moral Theory*, p. 168 and n. 59, for the latter.

from all the things which derive their beauty from it. It exists independently of all beautiful things, and nothing that happens to them can ever affect it. About the relationship between Beauty and the many beautiful things for whose beauty it is responsible and which it explains we learn nothing in the *Symposium* (or, for that matter, in the dialogues where the theory of Forms is given more systematic exposition: cf. *Phaedo* 100D). What we do learn is that, despite its many forms and various objects, all love—whether we know it or not—is directed at the very nature of Beauty. And so *erōs*, which we first approached as the desire to possess sexually the body of another person, turns out to be a desire for immortality, for wisdom, and for the contemplation of an object which is not in any way bodily or physical. Furthermore, only when a lover devotes himself to the pursuit of Beauty as a whole "will it become possible for him to give birth not to images of virtue . . . but to true virtue" (212A). Sexual desire, properly channeled, leads not simply to gratification but to the good life.

The end of Socrates' speech is radically different from anything that has preceded it: the whole atmosphere of Agathon's feast seems to have changed. But Plato does not allow this serious, almost hieratic mood to last for long. One of the greatest dramatic features of the *Symposium* is the way in which seriousness alternates with lightheartedness, instruction with banter, self-revelation with irony. And one of the work's most artful reversals occurs at the end of Socrates' speech, with the drunken entrance of Alcibiades, who does his best to turn the sober feast into a drinking contest (212C ff.).

The noise Alcibiades and his party make at Agathon's door is heard "all of a sudden" (*exaiphnēs*): Plato seems to be marking explicitly a reversal in the atmosphere which Diotima had created by her own reversal of the mood that had prevailed earlier when she introduced the Form of Beauty, which also, as we saw, comes "all of a sudden" into view (210E).[7] But even if Alcibiades' boisterous entrance seems hardly compatible with Diotima's rev-

---

7. The same word is used at 223B to mark the sudden entrance of an even drunker group, which brings about the disintegration of the party after the end of Alcibiades' speech.

elation (in fact, it seems to be quite the opposite), his contribution to the dialogue is as central as hers, and what he has to reveal is quite as important.

We have already seen that Diotima has argued that *erōs* should be conceived not on the model of the beloved but on that of the lover: he is neither beautiful nor totally ugly, but beauty's pursuer; he is neither wise nor foolish, but wisdom's admirer (*philosophos*); he is neither god nor mortal, but a "spirit" (*daimōn, daimonion*, 202D–203A). Now, throughout the *Symposium*, Socrates has been said to love beautiful young men and boys; he is the perfect philosopher; and he is even referred to as *daimonios* by Alcibiades (219C). This suggests that the model on which *erōs* is to be conceived is not so much the lover in general but Socrates in particular; after all, he has already admitted that "the only thing I say I understand is the art of love" (177D). At the same time, the identification of Socrates with the lover and with love itself suggests that Socrates is not the proper object of love: his role, like that of the lover and love itself, is that of the pursuer, not of the pursued.

And yet the matter is more complicated. As Alcibiades makes his way to Agathon's couch in order to crown Agathon with a wreath he has brought for that purpose, he fails to see that Socrates is also lying there. It is only after he is ready to lie down that Alcibiades finally becomes aware of Socrates, turns to him, and says, "You always do this to me—all of a sudden (*exaiphnēs*) you'll turn up out of nowhere where I least expect you!" (213C). Thus, after Socrates has been implicitly identified with love and the lover and while both he and Alcibiades seem to be in agreement over the fact that Socrates is the lover and Alcibiades his beloved, Alcibiades' language connects Socrates with Diotima's description of the ultimate object of love, the very Form of Beauty. This is a crucial point, but not much is made of it here. Plato seems to be placing what we will later be able to see as a subtle hint as to how we are to understand Socrates in this work. We shall return to it below.

Alcibiades is asked to make his own contribution to the praise of *erōs*, but he refuses because he claims that Socrates is too jealous for him to dare to praise anyone else in his presence. A great deal of good-natured banter about who is jealous of whom follows, and Eryximachus finally suggests that Alcibiades should speak in praise of Socrates, which he proceeds to do (215A ff.).

Given the subtle connections already established between Socrates and *erōs*, this is less of a change of subject than we might suppose. And in fact Alcibiades' witty encomium of Socrates develops a number of themes from Diotima's speech (which confirms that both speeches are Plato's creations). Socrates, he says, is like the statues of Silenus—far from beautiful on the outside but full of lovely little figures of the gods inside (215A−B). This shows Socrates to be neither perfectly beautiful nor totally ugly, and it also offers a concrete image of Diotima's metaphor of the lover's being pregnant "both in body and in soul." That he is a philosopher is, of course, the most obvious fact about him (218A−B), and Alcibiades returns again and again to the fact that Socrates is full of the best and most virtuous ideas and arguments (215B−216C, 221D−222A). And that he is almost superhuman is intimated not only by his incredible stamina and courage (219E−221C) but also by the comparison with Silenus, who was the semidivine companion of Dionysus and, as we have mentioned already, by Alcibiades' application to him of the word *daimonios*.

All these hints connecting Socrates with *erōs*, however, seem to be shaken by the conclusion of Alcibiades' speech. Alcibiades here mentions Socrates' "deception" (222A−B). What this deception is has been foreshadowed both by the use of "all of a sudden" at 213C and by another unobtrusive remark at 217C, where Alcibiades, describing his unsuccessful attempts to seduce Socrates, says that he invited him to dinner "as if *I* were his lover and he my young prey!" In his conclusion, Alcibiades comes out and accuses Socrates explicitly, and only half in jest, of a conscious and devious practice: "He has deceived us all: he presents himself as your lover, and, before you know it, you're in love with him yourself!"

We have now come full circle. Agathon's speech conceived and praised love as the beloved; Diotima identified love with the lover and, implicitly, with Socrates; Alcibiades, still thinking of Socrates as love, now reveals him to be, in reality, the beloved. But the circle has made a tremendous difference. Plato gives us in Socrates a union of lover and beloved, beguiler and beguiled.

But the personification of *erōs*'s two aspects in Socrates inevitably leads further. Unlike Agathon's unthinking love for love, which makes *erōs* an end in itself, to love Socrates, as Alcibiades knows and makes clear to the company, is to love what Socrates, as *erōs*, loves: the possession of beauty, wisdom, and goodness. To love Socrates is to be a philosopher. And, as we know from many of Plato's other Socratic dialogues, this is exactly what Socrates wanted of those he approached in his direct yet ironic manner.

This very serious point is made through the broad comedy that characterizes the whole episode of Alcibiades. But, of course, the point could not be made without the very serious speech of Diotima, which sets the stage for Alcibiades' antics. And Diotima's speech, in turn, depends crucially on a refutation of the views presented with the utmost elegance in Agathon's lovely trifle. The serious and the comic exist side by side in this dialogue, and each is equally crucial for the philosophical ideas the work communicates. That serious philosophy can be done at the same time that entertaining, even comic, events and conversations are depicted is not only true but may actually be the message with which the *Symposium* itself ends. Early into the morning hours, after everyone else has left or drifted off to sleep, Socrates is trying to prove to Agathon, the tragic poet, and to Aristophanes, who wrote comedies, that "the skillful tragic dramatist should also be a comic poet" (223D).

Whether this interpretation of the dialogue's end is or is not correct, the *Symposium* is a philosophical masterpiece because it is such a successful literary work. It presents a revisionary, otherworldly conception of love and a metaphysical vision to support that conception. But it is only by showing Socrates to be as much at home in everyday life as he is in the search for wisdom, as capable of being a good man here and now as he is devoted to the pursuit of a Beauty that does not exist in this world, as sturdy a drinker as he is an astute dialectician, that Plato has succeeded in convincing generations of readers that his idea of love is not simply a wild philosophical fantasy but rather an ideal according to which life can almost be lived. The various aspects of the dialogue do fit together after all. The *Symposium* is to be read and savored for all these reasons: for its philosophical views—the theory of love, the description of the Form of Beauty;

for its literary elements—the brightness of the occasion it de-
picts, the portrayal of the various speakers, the characterization
of Socrates; and for the product of the interaction between these
two—the demonstration that living according to that theory has
produced, whatever our misgivings, a hero of our culture.

NOTE ON
THE TRANSLATION

OUR AIM HAS BEEN to produce an idiomatic English version of the *Symposium* with some literary grace and appropriate variations in style. We have made no attempt to follow the fashion of rendering each Greek word consistently: words convey meaning not only because of the letters that make them up but also because of the context in which they appear. No single English word, for example, will do for the Greek word *kalos*. For this we have used "fine," "good," "beautiful," "noble" in Phaedrus' speech, "honorable" in Pausanias' speech, and both "good" and "beautiful" when Socrates is speaking. In Agathon's speech, to cite another case, *sophia* swings from "wisdom" to "skill" and back again. We have translated the word differently in different places, explaining the matter in the notes. Similarly, for the related word *technē* we have used "profession," "science," and "expertise." For *aischros* we have used "ugly," "bad," and "shameful." For *eudaimōn* we have had to settle for the weak and inaccurate "happy." Sometimes, where the Greek is simple, we have been compelled to be wordy; at other times the situation is reversed. In Agathon's speech, for example, we had to supply "and the effects he has on others are not forced" for *oute poiōn poiei* at 196C1. At 196D7, by contrast, we made things simpler: *hin' au kai egō* did not require translation at all.

INTRODUCTORY DIALOGUE

APOLLODORUS

I N FACT, YOUR QUESTION does not find me unprepared. 172A
Just the other day, as it happens, I was walking to the city
from my home in Phaleron when a man I know, who was
making his way behind me, saw me and called from a distance:

"The gentleman from Phaleron!" he yelled, trying to be
funny.[1] "Hey, Apollodorus, wait!"

So I stopped and waited.

"Apollodorus, I've been looking for you!" he said. "You know
there once was a gathering at Agathon's when Socrates, Alcibi- 172B
ades, and their friends had dinner together; I wanted to ask you
about the speeches they made on Love. What were they? I heard
a version from a man who had it from Phoenix, Philip's son, but
it was badly garbled, and he said you were the one to ask. So
please, will you tell me all about it? After all, Socrates is your
friend—who has a better right than you to report his conversation? But before you begin," he added, "tell me this: were you
there yourself?"

"Your friend must have really garbled his story," I replied, "if 172C
you think this affair was so recent that I could have been there."

"I did think that," he said.

"Glaucon, how could you? You know very well Agathon
hasn't lived in Athens for many years, while it's been less than
three that I've been Socrates' companion and made it my job to 173A
know exactly what he says and does each day. Before that, I
simply drifted aimlessly. Of course, I used to think that what I

---

1. The joke is that Athenians addressed each other in this fashion (by
the names of their demes) only on formal occasions, as in court. Cf.
Gorgias 495B.

was doing was important, but in fact I was the most worthless man on earth—as bad as you are this very moment: I used to think philosophy was the last thing a man should do."

"Stop joking, Apollodorus," he replied. "Just tell me when the party took place."

"When we were still children, when Agathon won the prize with his first tragedy. It was the day after he and his troupe held their victory celebration."

"So it really was a long time ago," he said. "Then who told you about it? Was it Socrates himself?"

173B "Oh, for god's sake, of course not!" I replied. "It was the very same man who told Phoenix, a fellow called Aristodemus, from Cydatheneum, a real runt of a man, who always went barefoot. He went to the party because, I think, he was obsessed with Socrates—one of the worst cases at that time. Naturally, I checked part of his story with Socrates, and Socrates agreed with his account."

"Please tell me, then," he said. "You speak and I'll listen, as we walk to the city. This is the perfect opportunity."

173C So this is what we talked about on our way; and that's why, as I said before, I'm not unprepared. Well, if I'm to tell *you* about it too—I'll be glad to. After all, my greatest pleasure comes from philosophical conversation, even if I'm only a listener, whether or not I think it will be to my advantage. All other talk, especially the talk of rich businessmen like you, bores me to tears, and I'm sorry for you and your friends because you think your affairs are

173D important when really they're totally trivial. Perhaps, in your turn, you think I'm a failure, and, believe me, I think that what you think is true. But as for all of you, I don't just *think* you are failures—I know it for a fact.

FRIEND

You'll never change, Apollodorus! Always nagging, even at yourself! I do believe you think everybody—yourself first of all—is totally worthless, except, of course, Socrates. I don't know exactly how you came to be called "the maniac," but you certainly talk like one, always furious with everyone, including yourself—but not with Socrates!

Well, if I could opine one way or the other I would but right now I'm just digesting.

APOLLODORUS

Of course, my dear friend, it's perfectly obvious why I have these views about us all: it's simply because I'm a maniac, and I'm raving!   *173E*

FRIEND

It's not worth arguing about this now, Apollodorus. Please do as I asked: tell me the speeches.

APOLLODORUS

All right . . . Well, the speeches went something like this—but I'd better tell you the whole story from the very beginning, as Aristodemus told it to me.   *174A*

He said, then, that one day he ran into Socrates, who had just bathed and put on his fancy sandals—both very unusual events. So he asked him where he was going, and why he was looking so good.

Socrates replied, "I'm going to Agathon's for dinner. I managed to avoid yesterday's victory party—I really don't like crowds—but I promised to be there today. So, naturally, I took great pains with my appearance: I'm going to the house of a good-looking man; I had to look my best. But let me ask you this," he added, "I know you haven't been invited to the dinner; how would you like to come anyway?"   *174B*

And Aristodemus answered, "I'll do whatever you say."

"Come with me, then," Socrates said, "and we shall prove the proverb wrong; the truth is, 'Good men go uninvited to Goodman's feast.'[2] Even Homer himself, when you think about it,

---

2. Agathon's name could be translated "Goodman." The proverb is, "Good men go uninvited to an inferior man's feast" (Eupolis fr. 289). Menelaus calls on Agamemnon at *Iliad* ii.408. Menelaus is called a limp spearman at xvii.587. For a different version of the proverb, see Hesiod, fr. 264.

174C did not much like this proverb; he not only disregarded it, he violated it. Agamemnon, of course, is one of his great warriors, while he describes Menelaus as a 'limp spearman.' And yet, when Agamemnon offers a sacrifice and gives a feast, Homer has the weak Menelaus arrive uninvited at his superior's table."

Aristodemus replied to this, "Socrates, I am afraid Homer's description is bound to fit me better than yours. Mine is a case of an obvious inferior arriving uninvited at the table of a man of letters. I think you'd better figure out a good excuse for bringing me along, because, you know, I won't admit I've come without an 174D invitation. I'll say I'm your guest."

"Let's go," he said. "We'll think about what to say 'as we proceed the two of us along the way.'"[3]

With these words, they set out. But as they were walking, Socrates began to think about something, lost himself in thought, and kept lagging behind. Whenever Aristodemus stopped to wait for him, Socrates would urge him to go on 174E ahead. When he arrived at Agathon's he found the gate wide open, and that, Aristodemus said, caused him to find himself in a very embarrassing situation: a household slave saw him the moment he arrived and took him immediately to the dining room, where the guests were already lying down on their couches, and dinner was about to be served.

As soon as Agathon saw him, he called:

"Welcome, Aristodemus! What perfect timing! You're just in time for dinner! I hope you're not here for any other reason—if you are, forget it. I looked all over for you yesterday, so I could invite you, but I couldn't find you anywhere. But where is Socrates? How come you didn't bring him along?"

So I turned around (Aristodemus said), and Socrates was nowhere to be seen. And I said that it was actually Socrates who had brought me along as his guest.

175A "I'm delighted he did," Agathon replied. "But where is he?"

---

3. An allusion to Homer, *Iliad* x.222–26. Plato quotes the same line more accurately at *Protagoras* 348D: "When two go together, one has an idea before the other."

"He was directly behind me, but I have no idea where he is now."

"Go look for Socrates," Agathon ordered a slave, "and bring him in. Aristodemus," he added, "you can share Eryximachus' couch."

A slave brought water, and Aristodemus washed himself before he lay down. Then another slave entered and said: "Socrates is here, but he's gone off to the neighbor's porch. He's standing there and won't come in even though I called him several times."

"How strange," Agathon replied. "Go back and bring him in. Don't leave him there."

But Aristodemus stopped him. "No, no," he said. "Leave him alone. It's one of his habits: every now and then he just goes off like that and stands motionless, wherever he happens to be. I'm sure he'll come in very soon, so don't disturb him; let him be."

"Well, all right, if you really think so," Agathon said, and turned to the slaves: "Go ahead and serve the rest of us. What you serve is completely up to you; pretend nobody's supervising you—as if I ever did! Imagine that we are all your own guests, myself included. Give us good reason to praise your service."

So they went ahead and started eating, but there was still no sign of Socrates. Agathon wanted to send for him many times, but Aristodemus wouldn't let him. And, in fact, Socrates came in shortly afterward, as he always did—they were hardly halfway through their meal. Agathon, who, as it happened, was all alone on the farthest couch, immediately called: "Socrates, come lie down next to me. Who knows, if I touch you, I may catch a bit of the wisdom that came to you under my neighbor's porch. It's clear you've seen the light. If you hadn't, you'd still be standing there."

Socrates sat down next to him and said, "How wonderful it would be, dear Agathon, if the foolish were filled with wisdom simply by touching the wise. If only wisdom were like water, which always flows from a full cup into an empty one when we connect them with a piece of yarn—well, then I would consider it the greatest prize to have the chance to lie down next to you. I would soon be overflowing with your wonderful wisdom. My own wisdom is of no account—a shadow in a dream—while yours is bright and radiant and has a splendid future. Why,

175B

175C

175D

175E

young as you are, you're so brilliant I could call more than thirty thousand Greeks as witnesses." 4

"Now you've gone *too* far, Socrates," Agathon replied. "Well, eat your dinner. Dionysus will soon enough be the judge of our claims to wisdom!"5

176A

Socrates took his seat after that and had his meal, according to Aristodemus. When dinner was over, they poured a libation to the god, sang a hymn, and—in short—followed the whole ritual. Then they turned their attention to drinking. At that point Pausanias addressed the group:

"Well, gentlemen, how can we arrange to drink less tonight? To be honest, I still have a terrible hangover from yesterday, and I could really use a break. I daresay most of you could, too, since you were also part of the celebration. So let's try not to overdo it."

176B

Aristophanes replied: "Good idea, Pausanias. We've got to make a plan for going easy on the drink tonight. I was over my head last night myself, like the others."

After that, up spoke Eryximachus, son of Akoumenos: "Well said, both of you. But I still have one question: How do *you* feel, Agathon? Are you strong enough for serious drinking?"

"Absolutely not," replied Agathon. "I've no strength left for anything."

176C

"What a lucky stroke for us," Eryximachus said, "for me, for Aristodemus, for Phaedrus, and the rest—that you large-capacity drinkers are already exhausted. Imagine how weak drinkers like ourselves feel after last night! Of course I don't include Socrates in my claims: he can drink or not, and will be satisfied whatever we do. But since none of us seems particularly eager to over-indulge, perhaps it would not be amiss for me to provide you with some accurate information as to the nature of intoxication.

176D

---

4. Socrates' style here is highly rhetorical and deeply ironic, as Agathon recognizes. Thirty thousand is the traditional number of male citizens in the assembly; the theater of Dionysus, however, where the tragic contests were held, accommodated no more than seventeen thousand spectators.

5. Dionysus was the god of wine and drunkenness. In fact, Agathon is unwittingly proved right, because the drunken Alcibiades will crown Socrates with the same ribbons he had earlier used to crown Agathon.

If I have learned anything from medicine, it is the following point: inebriation is harmful to everyone. Personally, therefore, I always refrain from heavy drinking; and I advise others against it—especially people who are suffering the effects of a previous night's excesses."

"Well," Phaedrus interrupted him, "I always follow your advice, especially when you speak as a doctor. In this case, if the others know what's good for them, they too will do just as you say."

At that point they all agreed not to get drunk that evening; *176E* they decided to drink only as much as pleased them.

"It's settled, then," said Eryximachus. "We are resolved to force no one to drink more than he wants. I would like now to make a further motion: let us dispense with the flute-girl who just made her entrance; let her play for herself or, if she prefers, for the women in the house. Let us instead spend our evening in conversation. If you are so minded, I would like to propose a subject." *177A*

They all said they were quite willing, and urged him to make his proposal. So Eryximachus said:

"Let me begin by citing Euripides' *Melanippe*: 'Not mine the tale.' What I am about to tell belongs to Phaedrus here, who is deeply indignant on this issue, and often complains to me about it:

" 'Eryximachus,' he says, 'isn't it an awful thing! Our poets have composed hymns in honor of just about any god you can think of; but has a single one of them given one moment's thought to the god of love, ancient and powerful as he is? As for *177B* our fancy intellectuals, they have written volumes praising Heracles and other heroes (as did the distinguished Prodicus). Well, perhaps *that's* not surprising, but I've actually read a book by an accomplished author who saw fit to extol the usefulness of salt! *177C* How *could* people pay attention to such trifles and never, not even once, write a proper hymn to Love? How could anyone ignore so great a god?'

"Now, Phaedrus, in my judgment, is quite right. I would like, therefore, to take up a contribution, as it were, on his behalf, and gratify his wish. Besides, I think this a splendid time for all of us here to honor the god. If you agree, we can spend the whole *177D* evening in discussion, because I propose that each of us give as good a speech in praise of Love as he is capable of giving, in proper order from left to right. And let us begin with Phaedrus, who is at the head of the table and is, in addition, the father of our subject."

"No one will vote against that, Eryximachus," said Socrates. "How could *I* vote 'No,' when the only thing I say I understand is the art of love?[6] Could Agathon and Pausanias? Could Aristophanes, who thinks of nothing but Dionysus and Aphrodite? No one I can see here now could vote against your proposal.

"And though it's not quite fair to those of us who have to speak last, if the first speeches turn out to be good enough and to exhaust our subject, I promise we won't complain. So let Phaedrus begin, with the blessing of Fortune; let's hear his praise of Love."

They all agreed with Socrates, and pressed Phaedrus to start. Of course, Aristodemus couldn't remember exactly what everyone said, and I myself don't remember everything he told me. But I'll tell you what he remembered best, and what I consider the most important points.

177E

178A

---

6. "The art of love": *ta erōtika*. See 198D1–2, 201D5, 207A5, 207C3, C7, 209E5 (where we have rendered it as "the rites of love"). A literal translation would be "erotics," as the formation is parallel to that of *ta physica* ("physics," or the science of nature) from *physis* ("nature"). In its usage in the *Symposium, ta erōtika* seems to range over both the science of love and the proper pursuit of love. On Socrates' claim to special knowledge in this area, see *Lysis* 204C and 206A.

THE SPEECH OF PHAEDRUS[7]

L OVE IS A GREAT GOD, wonderful in many ways to gods and men, and most marvelous of all is the way he came into being. We honor him as one of the most an- cient gods, and the proof of his great age is this: the parents of Love have no place in poetry or legend. According to Hesiod, the first to be born was Chaos,

178B

> . . . but then came
> Earth, broad-chested, a seat for all, forever safe,
> And Love.[8]

And Acousileos agrees with Hesiod: after Chaos came Earth and Love, these two.[9] And Parmenides tells of this beginning:

> The very first god [she] designed was Love.[10]

All sides agree, then, that Love is one of the most ancient gods. As such, he gives to us the greatest goods. I cannot say what greater good there is for a young boy than a gentle lover, or for a lover than a boy to love. There is a certain guidance each

178C

---

7. Phaedrus appears also in the *Protagoras* (at 315C) and in the *Phaedrus*, which is named after him, and which shows him as fascinated by speeches about love. It is noteworthy that all of the speakers in the *Symposium*, with the interesting exception of Aristophanes, appear in the *Protagoras*. For their shared interest in philosophy, see 218B.

8. *Theogony* 116–120, 118 omitted. The poet Hesiod was the first Greek writer to treat cosmology and the origins of things.

9. Acousileos was an early-fifth-century writer of genealogies.

10. Parmenides, B 13. "She," the unstated subject of "designed," is evidently the goddess of B 12.

9

person needs for his whole life, if he is to live well; and nothing
imparts this guidance—not high kinship, not public honor, not

178D   wealth—nothing imparts this guidance as well as Love. What
guidance do I mean? I mean a sense of shame at acting shame-
fully, and a sense of pride in acting well. Without these, nothing
fine or great can be accomplished, in public or in private.

What I say is this: if a man in love is found doing something
shameful, or accepting shameful treatment because he is a cow-
ard and makes no defense, then nothing would give him more
pain than being seen by the boy he loves—not even being seen

178E   by his father or his comrades. We see the same thing also in the
boy he loves, that he is especially ashamed before his lover when
he is caught in something shameful. If only there were a way to
start a city or an army made up of lovers and the boys they
love![11] Theirs would be the best possible system of society, for
they would hold back from all that is shameful, and seek honor

179A   in each other's eyes.[12] Even a few of them, in battle side by side,
would conquer all the world, I'd say. For a man in love would
never allow his loved one, of all people, to see him leaving ranks
or dropping weapons. He'd rather die a thousand deaths! And as
for leaving the boy behind, or not coming to his aid in danger—
why, no one is so base that true Love could not inspire him with

179B   courage, and make him as brave as if he'd been born a hero.[13]
When Homer says a god 'breathes might' into some of the heroes, this is really Love's gift to every lover.

Besides, no one will die for you but a lover, and a lover will
do this even if she's a woman. Alcestis is proof to everyone in
Greece that what I say is true.[14] Only she was willing to die in

---

11. Such an army, the "Sacred Band," was founded by Gorgides at
Thebes around 378 B.C. and was supposed to have remained undefeated
until wiped out at Chaeronea in 338 (Plutarch, *Pelopidas* 14 ff). The
implications of this for dating Plato's *Symposium* are discussed by H.B.
Mattingley in *Phronesis* 3 (1958) 31–39 and by Kenneth Dover in *Phronesis* 10 (1965) 1–20. Xenophon has Socrates criticize Pausanias for taking the Sacred Band as an ideal in his *Symposium* at viii.32–34.

12. Translating Ruecker's deletion of ἤ.

13. Cf. 180B.

14. Apollo gave Admetus a chance to live if anyone would go to Hades
in his place. Only Alcestis, the wife of Admetus, was willing to do this.

place of her husband, although his father and mother were still *179C*
alive. Because of her love, she went so far beyond his parents in
family feeling that she made them look like outsiders, as if they
belonged to their son in name only. And when she did this her
deed struck everyone, even the gods, as nobly done. The gods
were so delighted, in fact, that they gave her the prize they
reserve for a handful chosen from the throngs of noble heroes—
they sent her soul back from the dead. As you can see, the eager *179D*
courage of love wins highest honors from the gods.

Orpheus, however, they sent unsatisfied from Hades, after
showing him only an image of the woman he came for. They did
not give him the woman herself, because they thought he was
soft (he was, after all, a cithara-player) and did not dare to die
like Alcestis for Love's sake, but contrived to enter living into
Hades. So they punished him for that, and made him die at the
hands of women.[15] *179E*

The honor they gave to Achilles is another matter. They sent
him to the Isles of the Blest because he dared to stand by his
lover Patroclus and avenge him, even after he had learned from
his mother that he would die if he killed Hector, but that if he *180A*
chose otherwise he'd go home and end his life as an old man.
Instead he chose to die for Patroclus, and more than that, he did
it for a man whose life was already over. The gods were highly
delighted at this, of course, and gave him special honor, because
he made so much of his lover.[16] Aeschylus talks nonsense when

---

15. Orpheus was a musician of legendary powers, who charmed his
way into the underworld in search of his dead wife. Phaedrus' version
of this quest for Euridice is unique in antiquity; possibly we are to think
that he alters the legend to make his point. Earlier versions naturally
blamed Orpheus' death by Maenads on his treatment of Dionysus, as
Maenads were devoted to that god. Later versions say that he failed to
bring back Euridice because he could not refrain from turning back and
looking at her (Vergil *Georgics* 4.453 ff).
16. See the introduction, p. xv. The ancient Greeks thought of love as
asymmetrical, between an older lover and a younger loved one. The
loved one was not expected to love his lover. That Achilles, a nonlover,
should sacrifice his life for his lover Patroclus was thus extraordinary—
and, by the way, contradicts the maxim of 179B, "no one will die for you
but a lover."

he claims Achilles was the lover; he was more beautiful than Patroclus, more beautiful than all the heroes, and still beardless. Besides he was much younger, as Homer says.[17]

180B　　In truth, the gods honor virtue most highly when it belongs to Love. They are more impressed and delighted, however, and are more generous with a loved one who cherishes his lover, than with a lover who cherishes the boy he loves. A lover is more godlike than his boy, you see, since he is inspired by a god. That's why they gave a higher honor to Achilles than to Alcestis,[18] and sent him to the Isles of the Blest.

Therefore I say Love is the most ancient of the gods, the most honored, and the most powerful in helping men gain virtue and blessedness, whether they are alive or have passed away.

180C　　That was more or less what Phaedrus said according to Aristodemus. There followed several other speeches which he couldn't remember very well. So he skipped them and went directly to the speech of Pausanias.

Machiavelli blvd. to live rightly, one should continuously read ancient works — as such —

---

17. Achilles was the lover in Aeschylus' play, *The Myrmidons*. In Homer there is no hint of sexual attachment between Achilles and Patroclus.
18. The point is that Alcestis is treated in the story as a lover rather than as one who is loved, and so earns less honor than Achilles by her sacrifice. See 179B–C.

THE SPEECH OF PAUSANIAS[19]

PHAEDRUS (PAUSANIAS BEGAN), I'm not quite sure our subject has been well defined. Our charge has been simple—to speak in praise of Love. This would have been fine if Love himself were simple, too, but as a matter of fact, there are two kinds of Love. In view of this, it might be better to begin by making clear which kind of Love we are to praise. Let 180D me therefore try to put our discussion back on the right track and explain which kind of Love ought to be praised. Then I shall give him the praise he deserves, as the god he is.

It is a well-known fact that Love and Aphrodite are insepar-able. If, therefore, Aphrodite were a single goddess, there could also be a single Love; but, since there are actually two goddesses of that name, there also are two kinds of Love. I don't expect you'll disagree with me about the two goddesses, will you? One is an older deity, the motherless daughter of Uranus, the god of heaven: she is known as Urania, or Heavenly Aphrodite. The other goddess is younger, the daughter of Zeus and Dione: her name is Pandemos, or Common Aphrodite. It follows, therefore, 180E that there is a Common as well as a Heavenly Love, depending on which goddess is Love's partner. And although, of course, all the gods must be praised, we must still make an effort to keep these two gods apart.

The reason for this applies in the same way to every type of action: considered in itself, no action is either good or bad, honorable or shameful. Take, for example, our own case. We had 181A a choice between drinking, singing, or having a conversation.

---

19. Pausanias is mentioned in the *Protagoras* as a student of Prodicus (315D–E); this dialogue too treats Pausanias' love for Agathon as famous in Athens (cf. 198B). Pausanias' passionate defense of homosexuality is criticized in Xenophon's *Symposium* (viii.32–34).

Now, in itself none of these is better than any other: how it comes out depends entirely on how it is performed. If it is done honorably and properly, it turns out to be honorable; if it is done improperly, it is disgraceful. And my point is that exactly this principle applies to being in love: Love is not in himself noble and worthy of praise; that depends on whether the sentiments he produces in us are themselves noble.

181B   Now the Common Aphrodite's Love is himself truly common. As such, he strikes wherever he gets a chance. This, of course, is the love felt by the vulgar, who are attached to women no less than to boys, to the body more than to the soul, and to the least intelligent partners, since all they care about is completing the sexual act. Whether they do it honorably or not is of no concern. That is why they do whatever comes their way, sometimes good, sometimes bad; and which one it is is incidental to their purpose. For the Love who moves them belongs to a much younger goddess, who, through her parentage, partakes of the nature
181C   both of the female and the male.

Contrast this with the Love of Heavenly Aphrodite. This goddess, whose descent is purely male (hence this love is for boys), is considerably older and therefore free from the lewdness of youth. That's why those who are inspired by her Love are attracted to the male: they find pleasure in what is by nature stronger and more intelligent. But, even within the group that is attracted to handsome boys, some are not moved purely by this
181D   Heavenly Love; those who are do not fall in love with little boys; they prefer older ones whose cheeks are showing the first traces of a beard—a sign that they have begun to form minds of their own. I am convinced that a man who falls in love with a young man of this age is generally prepared to share everything with the one he loves—he is eager, in fact, to spend the rest of his own life with him. He certainly does not aim to deceive him—to take advantage of him while he is still young and inexperienced and then, after exposing him to ridicule, to move quickly on to
181E   someone else.

As a matter of fact, there should be a law forbidding affairs with young boys. If nothing else, all this time and effort would not be wasted on such an uncertain pursuit—and what is more uncertain than whether a particular boy will eventually make something of himself, physically or mentally? Good men, of course, are willing to make a law like this for themselves, but those other lovers, the vulgar ones, need external restraint. For just this reason we have placed every possible legal obstacle to their seducing our own wives and daughters. These vulgar *182A* lovers are the people who have given love such a bad reputation that some have gone so far as to claim that taking *any* man as a lover is in itself disgraceful. Would anyone make this claim if he weren't thinking of how hasty vulgar lovers are, and therefore how unfair to their loved ones? For nothing done properly and in accordance with our customs would ever have provoked such righteous disapproval.

I should point out, however, that, although the customs regarding Love in most cities are simple and easy to understand, here in Athens (and in Sparta as well) they are remarkably complex. In places where the people are inarticulate, like Elis or *182B* Boeotia, tradition straightforwardly approves taking a lover in every case. No one there, young or old, would ever consider it shameful. The reason, I suspect, is that, being poor speakers, they want to save themselves the trouble of having to offer reasons and arguments in support of their suits.

By contrast, in places like Ionia and almost every other part of the Persian empire, taking a lover is always considered disgraceful. The Persian empire is absolute; that is why it condemns love as well as philosophy and sport. It is no good for rulers if the *182C* people they rule cherish ambitions for themselves or form strong bonds of friendship with one another. That these are precisely the effects of philosophy, sport, and especially of Love is a lesson the tyrants of Athens learned directly from their own experience: Didn't their reign come to a dismal end because of the bonds uniting Harmodius and Aristogiton in love and affection?[20] *182D*

So you can see that plain condemnation of Love reveals lust for power in the rulers and cowardice in the ruled, while indiscriminate approval testifies to general dullness and stupidity.

Our own customs, which, as I have already said, are much

---

20. Harmodius and Aristogiton attempted to overthrow the tyrant Hippias in 514 B.C. Although their attempt failed, the tyranny fell three years later, and the lovers were celebrated as tyrannicides. The story is told by Thucydides, VI.54−59.

more difficult to understand, are also far superior. Recall, for example, that we consider it more honorable to declare your love rather than to keep it a secret, especially if you are in love with a youth of good family and accomplishment, even if he isn't all that beautiful. Recall also that a lover is encouraged in every possible way; this means that what he does is not considered shameful. On the contrary, conquest is deemed noble, and failure shame-

182E ful. And as for *attempts* at conquest, our custom is to praise lovers for totally extraordinary acts—so extraordinary, in fact,

183A that if they performed them for any other purpose whatever, they would reap the most profound contempt. Suppose, for example, that in order to secure money, or a public post, or any other practical benefit from another person, a man were willing to do what lovers do for the ones they love. Imagine that in pressing his suit he went to his knees in public view and begged in the most humiliating way, that he swore all sorts of vows, that he spent the night at the other man's doorstep, that he were anxious to provide services even a slave would have refused—well, you can be sure that everyone, his enemies no less than his

183B friends, would stand in his way. His enemies would jeer at his fawning servility, while his friends, ashamed on his behalf, would try everything to bring him back to his senses. But let a lover act in any of these ways, and everyone will immediately say what a charming man he is! No blame attaches to his behavior: custom treats it as noble through and through. And what is even more remarkable is that, at least according to popular wisdom, the gods will forgive a lover even for breaking his vows—a

183C lover's vow, our people say, is no vow at all. The freedom given to the lover by both gods and men according to our custom is immense.[21]

---

21. This is not true. Xenophon holds Pausanias up to criticism for over-stating the case for homosexuality, in his *Symposium*, at viii.34. Athenian custom condemned many manifestations of homosexuality. See Dover, *Greek Homosexuality*, especially pp. 104–107. For Plato's condemnation of the sexual act between males, see *Phaedrus* 250E (where he calls this an "unnatural pleasure") and 255E–56E as well as *Republic* 403B–C and *Laws* 636–37 and 838E (which forbids "homosexual relations that delib-erately wipe out the human race"). Plato does not represent this view as one his fellow Athenians would have found controversial.

In view of all this, you might well conclude that in our city we consider the lover's desire and the willingness to satisfy it as the noblest things in the world. When, on the other hand, you recall that fathers hire attendants for their sons as soon as they're old enough to be attractive, and that an attendant's main task is to prevent any contact between his charge and his suitors; when you recall how mercilessly a boy's own friends tease him if they catch him at it, and how strongly their elders approve and even encourage such mocking—when you take all this into account, *183D* you're bound to come to the conclusion that we Athenians consider such behavior the most shameful thing in the world.

In my opinion, however, the fact of the matter is this. As I said earlier, love is, like everything else, complex: considered simply in itself, it is neither honorable nor a disgrace—its character depends entirely on the behavior it gives rise to. To give oneself to a vile man in a vile way is truly disgraceful behavior; by contrast, it is perfectly honorable to give oneself honorably to the right man. Now you may want to know who counts as vile in this context. I'll tell you: it is the common, vulgar lover, who *183E* loves the body rather than the soul, the man whose love is bound to be inconstant, since what he loves is itself mutable and unstable. The moment the body is no longer in bloom, "he flies off and away,"[22] his promises and vows in tatters behind him. How different from this is a man who loves the right sort of character, and who remains its lover for life, attached as he is to something that is permanent. *184A*

We can now see the point of our customs: they are designed to separate the wheat from the chaff, the proper love from the vile. That's why we do everything we can to make it as easy as possible for lovers to press their suits and as difficult as possible for young men to comply; it is like a competition, a kind of test to determine to which sort each belongs. This explains two further facts: First, why we consider it shameful to yield too quickly: the passage of time in itself provides a good test in these matters. Second, why we also consider it shameful for a man to be seduced by money or political power, either because he *184B* cringes at ill-treatment and will not endure it or because, once he

---

22. *Iliad* ii.71.

has tasted the benefits of wealth and power, he will not rise above them. None of these benefits is stable or permanent, apart from the fact that no genuine affection can possibly be based upon them.

Our customs, then, provide for only one honorable way of taking a man as a lover. In addition to recognizing that the lover's total and willing subjugation to his beloved's wishes is neither servile nor reprehensible, we allow that there is one— and only one—further reason for willingly subjecting oneself to another which is equally above reproach: that is subjection for the sake of virtue. If someone decides to put himself at another's disposal because he thinks that this will make him better in wisdom or in any other part of virtue, we approve of his voluntary subjection: we consider it neither shameful nor servile. Both these principles—that is, both the principle governing the proper attitude toward the lover of young men and the principle governing the love of wisdom and of virtue in general—must be combined if a young man is to accept a lover in an honorable way. When an older lover and a young man come together and each obeys the principle appropriate to him—when the lover realizes that he is justified in doing anything for a loved one who grants him favors, and when the young man understands that he is justified in performing any service for a lover who can make him wise and virtuous—and when the lover *is* able to help the young man become wiser and better, and the young man *is* eager to be taught and improved by his lover—then, and only then, when these two principles coincide absolutely, is it ever honorable for a young man to accept a lover.

Only in this case, we should notice, is it never shameful to be deceived; in every other case it is shameful, both for the deceiver and the person he deceives. Suppose, for example, that someone thinks his lover is rich and accepts him for his money; his action won't be any less shameful if it turns out that he was deceived and his lover was a poor man after all. For the young man has already shown himself to be the sort of person who will do anything for money—and that is far from honorable. By the same token, suppose that someone takes a lover in the mistaken belief that this lover is a good man and likely to make him better himself, while in reality the man is horrible, totally lacking in virtue; even so, it is noble for him to have been deceived. For he too has demonstrated something about himself: that he is the sort of person who will do anything for the sake of virtue—and what could be more honorable than that? It follows, therefore, that giving in to your lover for virtue's sake is honorable, whatever the outcome. And this, of course, is the Heavenly Love of the heavenly goddess. Love's value to the city as a whole and to the citizens is immeasurable, for he compels the lover and his loved one alike to make virtue their central concern. All other *185C* forms of love belong to the vulgar goddess.

Phaedrus, I'm afraid this hasty improvisation will have to do as my contribution on the subject of Love.

When Pausanias finally came to a pause (I've learned this sort of fine figure from our clever rhetoricians), it was Aristophanes' turn, according to Aristodemus. But he had such a bad case of the hiccups—he'd probably stuffed himself again, though, of course, it could have been anything—that making a speech was totally out of the question. So he turned to the doctor, Eryximachus, who was next in line, and said to him: *185D*

"Eryximachus, it's up to you—as well it should be. Cure me or take my turn."

"As a matter of fact," Eryximachus replied, "I shall do both. I shall take your turn—you can speak in my place as soon as you feel better—and I shall also cure you. While I am giving my speech, you should hold your breath for as long as you possibly can. This may well eliminate your hiccups. If if fails, the best *185E* remedy is a thorough gargle. And if even this has no effect, then tickle your nose with a feather. A sneeze or two will cure even the most persistent case."

"The sooner you start speaking, the better," Aristophanes said. "I'll follow your instructions to the letter."

This, then, was the speech of Eryximachus:

THE SPEECH OF ERYXIMACHUS[23]

186A   PAUSANIAS INTRODUCED a crucial consideration in his speech, though in my opinion he did not develop it sufficiently. Let me therefore try to carry his argument to its logical conclusion. His distinction between the two species of Love seems to me very useful indeed. But if I have learned a single lesson from my own field, the science of medicine, it is that Love does not occur only in the human soul; it is not simply the attraction we feel toward human beauty: it is a significantly broader phenomenon. It certainly occurs within the animal king-

186B   dom, and even in the world of plants. In fact, it occurs everywhere in the universe. Love is a deity of the greatest importance: he directs everything that occurs, not only in the human domain, but also in that of the gods.

Let me begin with some remarks concerning medicine—I hope you will forgive my giving pride of place to my own profession. The point is that our very bodies manifest the two species of Love. Consider for a moment the marked difference, the radical dissimilarity, between healthy and diseased constitutions and the fact that dissimilar subjects desire and love objects that are themselves dissimilar. Therefore, the love manifested in health is fundamentally distinct from the love manifested in disease. And now recall that, as Pausanias claimed, it is as honorable to yield

186C   to a good man as it is shameful to consort with the debauched. Well, my point is that the case of the human body is strictly parallel. Everything sound and healthy in the body must be

---

23. Eryximachus' name is a pun on "belch-fighter"; he seems nevertheless to have been an historical character. His father Akoumenos is said by Xenophon to have a fine cure for loss of appetite: stop eating (*Memorabilia* iii.13.2). Eryximachus is a friend of Phaedrus (177A) and, like his father, a professional doctor (186E). In the *Protagoras* he is shown listening to the Sophist Hippias (315C).

encouraged and gratified; that is precisely the object of medicine. Conversely, whatever is unhealthy and unsound must be frustrated and rebuffed: that's what it is to be an expert in medicine.

In short, medicine is simply the science of the effects of Love on repletion and depletion of the body, and the hallmark of the *186D* accomplished physician is his ability to distinguish the Love that is noble from the Love that is ugly and disgraceful. A good practitioner knows how to affect the body and how to transform its desires; he can implant the proper species of Love when it is absent and eliminate the other sort whenever it occurs. The physician's task is to effect a reconciliation and establish mutual love between the most basic bodily elements. Which are those elements? They are, of course, those that are most opposed to one another, as hot is to cold, bitter to sweet, wet to dry, cases like those. In fact, our ancestor Asclepius first established medicine *186E* as a profession when he learned how to produce concord and love between such opposites—that is what those poet fellows say, and—this time—I concur with them.

Medicine, therefore, is guided everywhere by the god of *187A* Love, and so are physical education and farming as well. Further, a moment's reflection suffices to show that the case of poetry and music, too, is precisely the same. Indeed, this may have been just what Heraclitus had in mind, though his mode of expression certainly leaves much to be desired. The one, he says, "being at variance with itself is in agreement with itself" "like the attunement of a bow or a lyre."[24] Naturally, it is patently absurd to claim that an attunement or a harmony is in itself discordant or that its elements are still in discord with one another. Heraclitus probably meant that an expert musician creates a harmony by resolving the prior discord between high and low notes. For *187B* surely there can be no harmony so long as high and low are still discordant; harmony, after all, is consonance, and consonance is

---

24. Heraclitus of Ephesus, the early-fifth-century philosopher, was known for his enigmatic sayings. This one is quoted in a slightly different form by Hippolytus (Diels-Kranz B 51). Heraclitus seems to mean that the attunement of the lyre is achieved by the opposing tensions of string and instrument; if so, Eryximachus misses the point completely.

a species of agreement. Discordant elements, as long as they are still in discord, cannot come to an agreement, and they therefore cannot produce a harmony. Rhythm, for example, is produced

187C   only when fast and slow, though earlier discordant, are brought into agreement with each other. Music, like medicine, creates agreement by producing concord and love between these various opposites. Music is therefore simply the science of the effects of Love on rhythm and harmony.

These effects are easily discernible if you consider the constitution of rhythm and harmony in themselves; Love does not occur in both his forms in this domain. But the moment you consider, in their turn, the effects of rhythm and harmony on their

187D   audience—either through composition, which creates new verses and melodies, or through musical education, which teaches the correct performance of existing compositions—complications arise directly, and they require the treatment of a good practitioner. Ultimately, the identical argument applies once again: the love felt by good people or by those whom such love might improve in this regard must be encouraged and protected. This is the honorable, heavenly species of Love, produced by the mel-

187E   odies of Urania, the Heavenly Muse. The other, produced by Polyhymnia, the muse of many songs, is common and vulgar. Extreme caution is indicated here: we must be careful to enjoy his pleasures without slipping into debauchery—this case, I might add, is strictly parallel to a serious issue in my own field, namely, the problem of regulating the appetite so as to be able to enjoy a fine meal without unhealthy aftereffects.

In music, therefore, as well as in medicine and in all the other domains, in matters divine as well as in human affairs, we must attend with the greatest possible care to these two species of

188A   Love, which are, indeed, to be found everywhere. Even the seasons of the year exhibit their influence. When the elements to which I have already referred—hot and cold, wet and dry—are animated by the proper species of Love, they are in harmony with one another: their mixture is temperate, and so is the climate. Harvests are plentiful; men and all other living things are in good health; no harm can come to them. But when the sort of Love that is crude and impulsive controls the seasons, he brings

188B   death and destruction. He spreads the plague and many other diseases among plants and animals; he causes frost and hail and blights. All these are the effects of the immodest and disordered species of Love on the movements of the stars and the seasons of the year, that is, on the objects studied by the science called astronomy.

Consider further the rites of sacrifice and the whole area with which the art of divination is concerned, that is, the interaction *188C* between men and gods. Here, too, Love is the central concern: our object is to try to maintain the proper kind of Love and to attempt to cure the kind that is diseased. For what is the origin of all impiety? Our refusal to gratify the orderly kind of Love, and our deference to the other sort, when we should have been guided by the former sort of Love in every action in connection with our parents, living or dead, and with the gods. The task of divination is to keep watch over these two species of Love and to doctor them as necessary. Divination, therefore, is the practice that produces loving affection between gods and men; it is sim- *188D* ply the science of the effects of Love on justice and piety.

Such is the power of Love—so varied and great that in all cases it might be called absolute. Yet even so it is far greater when Love is directed, in temperance and justice, toward the good, whether in heaven or on earth: happiness and good fortune, the bonds of human society, concord with the gods above—all these are among his gifts.

Perhaps I, too, have omitted a great deal in this discourse on Love. If so, I assure you, it was quite inadvertent. And if in fact *188E* I have overlooked certain points, it is now your task, Aristophanes, to complete the argument—unless, of course, you are planning on a different approach. In any case, proceed; your hiccups seem cured. *189A*

Then Aristophanes took over (so Aristodemus said): "The hiccups have stopped all right—but not before I applied the Sneeze Treatment to them. Makes me wonder whether the 'orderly sort of Love' in the body calls for the sounds and itchings that constitute a sneeze, because the hiccups stopped immediately when I applied the Sneeze Treatment."

"You're good, Aristophanes," Eryximachus answered. "But watch what you're doing. You are making jokes before your

speech, and you're forcing me to prepare for you to say something funny, and to put up my guard against you, when other-

189B   wise you might speak at peace."

Then Aristophanes laughed. "Good point, Eryximachus. So
let me 'unsay what I have said.' But don't put up your guard. I'm
not worried about saying something funny in my coming oration. That would be pure profit, and it comes with the territory
of my Muse. What I'm worried about is that I might say something ridiculous."

"Aristophanes, do you really think you can take a shot at me,
and then escape? Use your head! Remember, as you speak, that
you will be called upon to give an account. Though perhaps, if I

189C   decide to, I'll let you off."

"Eryximachus," Aristophanes said, "indeed I do have in
mind a different approach to speaking than the one the two of
you used, you and Pausanias. You see, I think people have entirely missed the power of Love, because, if they had grasped it,
they'd have built the greatest temples and altars to him and
made the greatest sacrifices. But as it is, none of this is done for
him, though it should be, more than anything else! For he loves

189D   the human race more than any other god, he stands by us in our
troubles, and he cures those ills we humans are most happy to
have mended. I shall, therefore, try to explain his power to you;
and you, please pass my teaching on to everyone else."

STOP

THE SPEECH OF ARISTOPHANES[25]

F IRST YOU MUST LEARN what Human Nature was in the beginning and what has happened to it since, because long ago our nature was not what it is now, but very different. There were three kinds of human beings, that's my first point—not two as there are now, male and female. In addition to these, there was a third, a combination of those two; its name survives, though the kind itself has vanished. At that time, you see, the word "androgynous" really meant something: a form made up of male and female elements, though now there's nothing but the word, and that's used as an insult. My second point is that the shape of each human being was completely round, with back and sides in a circle; they had four hands each, as many legs as hands, and two faces, exactly alike, on a rounded neck. Between the two faces, which were on opposite sides, was one head with four ears. There were two sets of sexual organs, and everything else was the way you'd imagine it from what I've told you. They walked upright, as we do now, whatever direction they wanted. And whenever they set out to run fast, they thrust out all their eight limbs, the ones they had then, and spun rapidly, the way gymnasts do cartwheels, by bringing their legs around straight.

189E

190A

Now here is why there were three kinds, and why they were as I described them: The male kind was originally an offspring of the sun, the female of the earth, and the one that combined both genders was an offspring of the moon, because the moon shares

190B

---

25. Aristophanes (ca. 450–ca. 385 B.C.) was the famous writer of comedy who satirized Socrates unmercifully in *The Clouds*, on which see Socrates' reaction in the *Apology* at 18D. Here in the *Symposium*, somewhat surprisingly, Plato shows no ill will towards Aristophanes, but supplies him with a masterpiece, an inventive speech that is comic and seriously moving at the same time.

"...If my Soul has a shape, [it] will then it is An Elipse."

in both. They were spherical, and so was their motion, because they were like their parents in the sky.

In strength and power, therefore, they were terrible, and they had great ambitions. They made an attempt on the gods, and Homer's story about Ephialtes and Otos was originally about them: how they tried to make an ascent to heaven so as to attack

190C the gods.[26] Then Zeus and the other gods met in council to discuss what to do, and they were sore perplexed. They couldn't wipe out the human race with thunderbolts and kill them all off, as they had the giants, because that would wipe out the worship they receive, along with the sacrifices we humans give them. On the other hand, they couldn't let them run riot. At last, after great effort, Zeus had an idea.

"I think I have a plan," he said, "that would allow human beings to exist and stop their misbehaving: they will give up

190D being wicked when they lose their strength. So I shall now cut each of them in two. At one stroke they will lose their strength and also become more profitable to us, owing to the increase in their number. They shall walk upright on two legs. But if I find they still run riot and do not keep the peace," he said, "I will cut them in two again, and they'll have to make their way on one leg, hopping."

190E So saying, he cut those human beings in two, the way people cut sorb-apples before they dry them or the way they cut eggs with hairs. As he cut each one, he commanded Apollo to turn its face and half its neck towards the wound, so that each person would see that he'd been cut and keep better order. Then Zeus commanded Apollo to heal the rest of the wound, and Apollo did turn the face around, and he drew skin from all sides over what is now called the stomach, and there he made one mouth, as in a pouch with a drawstring, and fastened it at the center of the stomach. This is now called the navel. Then he smoothed out

191A the other wrinkles, of which there were many, and he shaped the breasts, using some such tool as shoemakers have for smoothing wrinkles out of leather on the form. But he left a few wrinkles around the stomach and the navel, to be a reminder of what happened long ago.

---

26. *Iliad* v. 385, *Odyssey* xii.308.

Now, since their natural form had been cut in two, each one longed for its own other half, and so they would throw their arms about each other, weaving themselves together, wanting to grow together. In that condition they would die from hunger and general idleness, because they would not do anything apart *191B* from each other. Whenever one of the halves died and one was left, the one that was left still sought another and wove itself together with that. Sometimes the half he met came from a woman, as we'd call her now, sometimes it came from a man; either way, they kept on dying.

Then, however, Zeus took pity on them, and came up with another plan: he moved their genitals around to the front! Before then, you see, they used to have their genitals outside, like their faces, and they cast seed and made children, not in one another, *191C* but in the ground, like cicadas. So Zeus brought about this re-location of genitals, and in doing so he invented interior repro-duction, *by* the man *in* the woman. The purpose of this was so that, when a man embraced a woman, he would cast his seed and they would have children; but when male embraced male, they would at least have the satisfaction of intercourse, after which they could stop embracing, return to their jobs, and look after their other needs in life. This, then, is the source of our *191D* desire to love each other. Love is born into every human being; it calls back the halves of our original nature together; it tries to make one out of two and heal the wound of human nature.

Each of us, then, is a "matching half" of a human whole, because each was sliced like a flatfish, two out of one, and each of us is always seeking the half that matches him. That's why a man who is split from the double sort (which used to be called "androgynous") runs after women. Many lecherous men have come from this class, and so do the lecherous women who run *191E* after men. Women who are split from a woman, however, pay no attention at all to men; they are oriented more towards women, and lesbians come from this class. People who are split from a male are male-oriented. While they are boys, because they are chips off the male block, they love men and enjoy lying with men and being embraced by men; those are the best of boys and *192A* lads, because they are the most manly in their nature. Of course, some say such boys are shameless, but they're lying. It's not because they have no shame that such boys do this, you see, but

because they are bold and brave and masculine, and they tend to
cherish what is like themselves. Do you want me to prove it?
Look, these are the only kind of boys who grow up to be politi-

192B   cians. When they're grown men, they are lovers of young men,
and they naturally pay no attention to marriage or to making
babies, except insofar as they are required by local custom. They,
however, are quite satisfied to live their lives with one another
unmarried. In every way, then, this sort of man grows up as a
lover of young men and a lover of Love, always rejoicing in his
own kind.

And so, when a person meets the half that is his very own,
whatever his orientation, whether it's to young men or not, then
something wonderful happens: the two are struck from their

192C   senses by love, by a sense of belonging to one another, and by
desire, and they don't want to be separated from one another,
not even for a moment.

These are the people who finish out their lives together and
still cannot say what it is they want from one another. No one
would think it is the intimacy of sex—that mere sex is the reason
each lover takes so great and deep a joy in being with the other.

192D   It's obvious that the soul of every lover longs for something else;
his soul cannot say what it is, but like an oracle it has a sense of
what it wants, and like an oracle it hides behind a riddle. Suppose two lovers are lying together and Hephaestus[27] stands over
them with his mending tools, asking, "What is it you human
beings really want from each other?" And suppose they're perplexed, and he asks them again: "Is this your heart's desire,
then—for the two of you to become parts of the same whole, as
near as can be, and never to separate, day or night? Because if
that's your desire, I'd like to weld you together and join you into
something that is naturally whole, so that the two of you are

192E   made into one. Then the two of you would share one life, as long
as you lived, because you would be one being, and by the same
token, when you died, you would be one and not two in Hades,
having died a single death. Look at your love, and see if this is

---

27. Hephaestus in Greek mythology is the craftsman god.

what you desire: wouldn't this be all the good fortune you could want?"

Surely you can see that no one who received such an offer would turn it down; no one would find anything else that he wanted. Instead, everyone would think he'd found out at last what he had always wanted: to come together and melt together with the one he loves, so that one person emerged from two. Why should this be so? It's because, as I said, we used to be complete wholes in our original nature, and now "Love" is the name for our pursuit of wholeness, for our desire to be complete.   *193A*

Long ago we were united, as I said; but now the god has divided us as punishment for the wrong we did him, just as the Spartans divided the Arcadians.[28] So there's a danger that if we don't keep order before the gods, we'll be split in two again, and then we'll be walking around in the condition of people carved on gravestones in bas-relief, sawn apart between the nostrils, like half dice. We should encourage all men, therefore, to treat the gods with all due reverence, so that we may escape this fate and   *193B* find wholeness instead. And we will, if Love is our guide and our commander. Let no one work against him. Whoever opposes Love is hateful to the gods, but if we become friends of the god and cease to quarrel with him, then we shall find the young men that are meant for us and win their love, as very few men do nowadays.

Now don't get ideas, Eryximachus, and turn this speech into a comedy. Don't think I'm pointing this at Pausanias and Agathon.   *193C* Probably, they both do belong to the group that are entirely masculine in nature. But I am speaking about everyone, men and women alike, and I say there's just one way for the human race to flourish: we must bring love to its perfect conclusion, and each of us must win the favors of his very own young man, so that he can recover his original nature. If that is the ideal, then,

---

28. Arcadia included the city of Mantinea, which opposed Sparta, and was rewarded for this by having its population divided and dispersed in 385 B.C. See Xenophon, *Hellenica* v.2.5–7.

of course, the nearest approach to it is best in present circum-
stances, and that is to win the favor of young men who are
naturally sympathetic to us.[29]

193D   If we are to give due praise to the god who can give us this
blessing, then, we must praise Love. Love does the best that can
be done for the time being: he draws us towards what belongs to
us. But for the future, Love promises the greatest hope of all: if
we treat the gods with due reverence, he will restore to us our
original nature, and by healing us, he will make us blessed and
happy.

         "That," he said, "is my speech about Love, Eryximachus. It is
rather different from yours. As I begged you earlier, don't make a
comedy of it. I'd prefer to hear what all the others will say—or,
193E   rather, what each of them will say, since Agathon and Socrates
are the only ones left."

         "I found your speech delightful," said Eryximachus, "so I'll
do as you say. Really, we've had such a rich feast of speeches on
Love, that if I couldn't vouch for the fact that Socrates and
Agathon are masters of the art of love, I'd be afraid that they'd
have nothing left to say. But as it is, I have no fears on this score."

194A   Then Socrates said, "That's because *you* did beautifully in the
contest, Eryximachus. But if you ever get in my position, or
rather the position I'll be in after Agathon's spoken so well, then
you'll really be afraid. You'll be at your wit's end, as I am now."

         "You're trying to bewitch me, Socrates," said Agathon, "by
making me think the audience expects great things of my
194B   speech, so I'll get flustered."

         "Agathon!" said Socrates, "How forgetful do you think I am?
I saw how brave and dignified you were when you walked right
up to the theater platform along with the actors and looked
straight out at that enormous audience. You were about to put
your own writing on display, and you weren't the least bit pan-
icked. After seeing that, how could I expect you to be flustered
by us, when we are so few?"

---

29. Aristophanes began at 193C3 to speak to all men and women, but at
C4 and C7 he plainly reverts to the idiom of homosexual love that suits
his audience.

"Why, Socrates," said Agathon. "You must think I have nothing but theater audiences on my mind! So you suppose I don't realize that, if you're intelligent, you find a few sensible men much more frightening than a senseless crowd?"

"No," he said, "It wouldn't be very handsome of me to think   194C
you crude in any way, Agathon. I'm sure that if you ever run into people you consider wise, you'll pay more attention to them than to ordinary people. But you can't suppose we're in that class; we were at the theater too, you know, part of the ordinary crowd. Still, if you did run into any wise men, other than yourself, you'd certainly be ashamed at the thought of doing anything ugly in front of them. Is that what you mean?"

"That's true," he said.

"On the other hand, you wouldn't be ashamed to do something ugly in front of ordinary people. Is that it?"   194D

At that point Phaedrus interrupted: "Agathon, my friend, if you answer Socrates, he'll no longer care whether we get anywhere with what we're doing here, so long as he has a partner for discussion. Especially if he's handsome. Now, like you, I enjoy listening to Socrates in discussion, but it is my duty to see to the praising of Love and to exact a speech from every one of this group. When each of you two has made his offering to the god, then you can have your discussion."   194E

"You're doing a beautiful job, Phaedrus," said Agathon. "There's nothing to keep me from giving my speech. Socrates will have many opportunities for discussion later."

THE SPEECH OF AGATHON[30]

I WISH FIRST TO SPEAK of how I ought to speak, and only then to speak. In my opinion, you see, all those who have spoken before me did not so much celebrate the god as congratulate human beings on the good things that come to them from the god. But who it is who gave these gifts, what he is like—no one has spoken about that. Now, only one method is correct for every praise, no matter whose: you must explain what qualities in the subject of your speech enable him to give the benefits for which we praise him. So now, in the case of Love, it is right for us to praise him first for what he is and afterwards for his gifts.

195A

I maintain, then, that while all the gods are happy, Love—if I may say so without giving offence—is the happiest of them all, for he is the most beautiful and the best. His great beauty lies in this: First, Phaedrus, he is the youngest of the gods.[31] He proves my point himself by fleeing old age in headlong flight, fast-moving though it is (that's obvious—it comes after us faster than it should). Love was born to hate old age and will come nowhere near it. Love always lives with young people and is one of them: the old story holds good that like is always drawn to like. And

195B

---

30. Agathon, the writer of tragedies, was famous for his personal beauty, for the originality of his plays, and for the influence on his writing of Sophistic rhetoric. Plato's *Protagoras* (315D−E) shows him listening to the Sophist Prodicus, and the speech here shows him to have been a disciple of Gorgias' style in rhetoric. Aristophanes satirized his style in the *Thesmophoriazousai* (101 ff) and speaks of his effeminacy (191−92). All Athens apparently knew that he was loved by Pausanias (see note 19).
31. See 178B.

though on many other points I agree with Phaedrus, I do not agree with this: that Love is more ancient than Kronos and Iapetos. No, I say that he is the youngest of the gods and stays *195C* young forever.

Those old stories Hesiod and Parmenides tell about the gods—those things happened under Necessity, not Love, if what they say is true. For not one of all those violent deeds would have been done—no castrations, no imprisonments—if Love had been present among them. There would have been peace and brotherhood instead, as there has been now as long as Love has been king of the gods.

So he is young. And besides being young, he is delicate. It *195D* takes a poet as good as Homer to show how delicate the god is. For Homer says that Mischief is a god and that she is delicate— well, that her feet are delicate, anyway! He says:

> . . . hers are delicate feet: not on the ground
> Does she draw nigh; she walks instead upon the heads of men.[32]

A lovely proof, I think, to show how delicate she is: she doesn't walk on anything hard; she walks only on what is soft. We shall *195E* use the same proof about Love, then, to show that he is delicate. For he walks not on earth, not even on people's skulls, which are not really soft at all, but in the softest of all the things that are, there he walks, there he has his home. For he makes his home in the characters, in the souls, of gods and men—and not even in every soul that comes along: when he encounters a soul with a harsh character, he turns away; but when he finds a soft and gentle character, he settles down in it. Always, then, he is touch- ing with his feet and with the whole of himself what is softest in the softest places. He must therefore be most delicate. *196A*

He is youngest, then, and most delicate; in addition he has a fluid, supple shape. For if he were hard, he would not be able to enfold a soul completely or escape notice when he first entered it or withdrew. Besides, his graceful good looks prove that he is balanced and fluid in his nature. Everyone knows that Love has

---

32. *Iliad* xix.92−93. "Mischief" translates *atē*.

extraordinary good looks, and between ugliness and Love there is unceasing war.[33]

And the exquisite coloring of his skin! The way the god consorts with flowers shows that. For he never settles in anything, *196B* be it a body or a soul, that cannot flower or has lost its bloom. His place is wherever it is flowery and fragrant; there he settles, there he stays.

Enough for now about the beauty of the god, though much remains still to be said. After this, we should speak of Love's moral character.[34] The main point is that Love is neither the cause nor the victim of any injustice; he does no wrong to gods or men, nor they to him. If anything has an effect on him, it is *196C* never by violence, for violence never touches Love. And the effects he has on others are not forced, for every service we give to love we give willingly. And whatever one person agrees on with another, when both are willing, that is right and just; so say "the laws that are kings of society."[35]

And besides justice, he has the biggest share of moderation.[36]

---

33. Here and at 195B Agathon is probably poking fun at the man who shares his couch—Socrates. Now long past his youth and never good-looking, Socrates is nevertheless no stranger to love, as everyone present knows.

34. "Moral character": *aretē*. Justice, Moderation, Bravery, and Wisdom are four cardinal virtues (excellences of character), the same four that Socrates will treat in the *Republic*. Here Agathon methodically covers all four in his encomium, assigning them to Love on the basis of a series of palpable confusions: Justice he equates wrongly with nonviolence, courage and moderation with power, wisdom with technical skill.

35. "The laws that are kings of society": a proverbial expression attributed by Aristotle to the fourth-century liberal thinker and rhetorician Alcidamas (*Rhetoric* 1406A17–23).

36. "Moderation": *sophrosunē*. The word can be translated also as "temperance" and, most literally, "sound-mindedness." It is often wrongly translated as "self-control." Plato and Aristotle generally contrast *sophrosunē* as a virtue with self-control: the person with *sophrosunē* is naturally well-tempered in every way and so does not need to control himself, or hold himself back. Here Agathon plays on the idea of self-control, losing the sense in which *sophrosunē* is a real excellence of character. In any event, *sophrosunē* is not the sort of thing that one could have "the biggest share of." The passage is meant in fun.

For moderation, by common agreement, is power over pleasures and passions, and no pleasure is more powerful than Love! But if they are weaker, they are under the power of Love, and *he* has the power; and because he has power over pleasures and passions, Love is exceptionally moderate.

And as for manly bravery, "Not even Ares can stand up to" Love![37] For Ares has no hold on Love, but Love does on Ares— love of Aphrodite, so runs the tale.[38] But he who has hold is more powerful than he who is held; and so, because Love has power over the bravest of the others, he is bravest of them all.   *196D*

Now I have spoken about the god's justice, moderation, and bravery; his wisdom remains.[39] I must try not to leave out anything that can be said on this. In the first place—to honor *our* profession as Eryximachus did his[40]—the god is so skilled a poet that he can make others into poets: once Love touches him, *anyone* becomes a poet,   *196E*

> . . . *howe'er uncultured he had been before.*[41]

This, we may fittingly observe, testifies that Love is a good poet, good, in sum, at every kind of artistic production. For you can't give to another what you don't have yourself, and you can't teach what you don't know.   *197A*

And as to the production of animals—who will deny that they are all born and begotten through Love's skill?

And as for artisans and professionals—don't we know that whoever has this god for a teacher ends up in the light of fame,

---

37. From Sophocles, fragment 235: "Even Ares cannot withstand Necessity." Ares is the god of war. Here Agathon treats Courage (*andreia*) simply as the ability to win a contest.

38. See *Odyssey* viii.266–366. Aphrodite's husband Hephaestus made a snare that caught Ares in bed with Aphrodite.

39. "Wisdom" translates *sophia,* which in Agathon's usage is roughly equivalent to *technē* (professional skill), and refers mainly to the ability to produce things, an ability which should not in itself be counted an excellence of character. We have accordingly used "wisdom" to translate *sophia* in the first instance; afterwards in this passage it is "skill" or "art."

40. See 186B, where Eryximachus gives pride of place to the art of medicine.

41. Euripides, fr 663, *Stheneboea;* quoted also at *Wasps* 1074.

while a man untouched by Love ends in obscurity? Apollo, for one, invented archery, medicine, and prophecy when desire and love[42] showed the way. Even he, therefore, would be a pupil of Love, and so would the Muses in music, Hephaestus in bronze work, Athena in weaving, and Zeus in "the governance of gods and men."[43]

That too is how the gods' quarrels were settled, once Love came to be among them—love of beauty, obviously, because love is not drawn to ugliness. Before that, as I said in the beginning,[44] and as the poets say, many dreadful things happened among the gods, because Necessity was king. But once this god was born, all goods came to gods and men alike through love of beauty.

This is how I think of Love, Phaedrus: first, he is himself the most beautiful and the best; after that, if anyone else is at all like that, Love is responsible. I am suddenly struck by a need to say something in poetic meter,[45] that it is he who—

197B

197C

---

42. The desire, evidently, is simply for success in each of these *technai* (see Dover *ad loc.*). "Love" is used as equivalent to desire, to facilitate the slide to "Love is the teacher." By this equivocating line of reasoning, Love would be the teacher of anyone who desired to learn.

Contrast this with Pausanias' speech (where the love that teaches is between a suitable role model and an aspiring youth) and with Socrates' speech (where it is love of absolute Beauty, manifesting itself first in love for a boy).

43. The construction is unusual, and this has suggested to most editors that this is another quotation from poetry, but we can only speculate as to the source.

44. 195C.

45. The lines that follow (197C5−197E5) are Agathon's own composition; they are an extreme parody of the style introduced by the Sophist Gorgias, whose exciting method of speaking had taken Athens by storm about ten years before the dramatic date of this dialogue.

The speech displays a rich variety of lyric meters, and is laced with internal rhymes, balanced phrases, and the other poetic devices Gorgias taught his students to use in formal speaking. It is in fact notably more poetical in its use of meter than the examples we have from Gorgias, as Dover points out. This invites us to think of the passage as a parody not only of Gorgias, but of Agathon's own style as well, in the parts of his tragedies that were in lyric meters. See the similar passage in the encomium by Gorgias on Athenian war heroes (fragment B6), and the parody of Agathon in Aristophanes' *Thesmophoriazousai*, 101 ff.

> *Gives peace to men and stillness to the sea,*
> *Lays winds to rest, and careworn men to sleep.*   197D

Love fills us with togetherness and drains all of our divisiveness
away. Love calls gatherings like these together. In feasts, in
dances, and in ceremonies, he gives the lead. Love moves us to
mildness, removes from us wildness. He is giver of kindness,
never of meanness. Gracious, kindly[46]—let wise men see and
gods admire! Treasure to lovers, envy to others, father of elegance, luxury, delicacy, grace, yearning, desire. Love cares well
for good men, cares not for bad ones. In pain, in fear, in desire,
or speech, Love is our best guide and guard; he is our comrade   197E
and our savior. Ornament of all gods and men, most beautiful
leader and the best! Every man should follow Love, sing beautifully his hymns, and join with him in the song he sings that
charms the mind of god or man.

This, Phaedrus, is the speech I have to offer. Let it be dedicated to the god, part of it in fun, part of it moderately serious,
as best I could manage.   198A

When Agathon finished, Aristodemus said, everyone there
burst into applause, so becoming to himself[47] and to the god did
they think the young man's speech.

Then Socrates glanced at Eryximachus and said, "Now do
you think I was foolish to feel the fear I felt before?[48] Didn't I
speak like a prophet a while ago when I said that Agathon would
give an amazing speech and I would be tongue-tied?"

"You were prophetic about one thing, I think," said Eryximachus, "that Agathon would speak well. But you, tongue-tied?
No, I don't believe that."   198B

"Bless you," said Socrates. "How am I not going to be
tongue-tied, I or anyone else, after a speech delivered with such
beauty and variety? The other parts may not have been so wonderful, but that at the end! Who would not be struck dumb on

---

46. Dover prints Usener's emendation of ἀγανός for ἀγαθός, and we
have translated this.
47. "To himself": as the youngest and best-looking man present, he has
"appropriately" emphasized youth and good looks.
48. By playing with "fear" in this way, Socrates makes fun of the allit-
erative style Agathon has been using at the end of his speech.

hearing the beauty of the words and phrases? Anyway, I was
worried that I'd not be able to say anything that came close to

198C   them in beauty, and so I would almost have run away and es-
caped, if there had been a place to go. And, you see, the speech
reminded me of Gorgias, so that I actually experienced what
Homer describes: I was afraid that Agathon would end by send-
ing the Gorgian head,[49] awesome at speaking in a speech,
against my speech, and this would turn me to stone by striking
me dumb. Then I realized how ridiculous I'd been to agree to

198D   join with you in praising Love and to say that I was a master of
the art of love, when I knew nothing whatever of this business,
of how anything whatever ought to be praised.[50] In my foolishness, I thought you should tell the truth about whatever you
praise, that this should be your basis, and that from this a
speaker should select the most beautiful truths and arrange
them most suitably. I was quite vain, thinking that I would talk
well[51] and that I knew the truth about praising anything whatever. But now it appears that this is not what it is to praise

198E   anything whatever; rather, it is to apply to the object the grand-
est and the most beautiful qualities, whether he actually has
them or not. And if they are false, that is no objection; for the
proposal, apparently, was that everyone here make the rest of us
think he is praising Love—and not that he actually praise him. I
think that is why you stir up every word and apply it to Love;

199A   your description of him and his gifts is designed to make him
look better and more beautiful than anything else—to ignorant
listeners, plainly, for of course he wouldn't look that way to those
who knew. And your praise did seem beautiful and respectful.

---

49. "Gorgian head" is a pun on "Gorgon's head." Agathon had par-
odied the style of Gorgias, and this style was considered to be irresisti-
bly powerful. According to mythology, the sight of a Gorgon's head
(such as Medusa's) would turn a man to stone. Homer tells of the threat
of a Gorgon's head to Odysseus (*Odyssey* xi.633–35).
50. Rhetoric as practiced by Gorgias and his followers was famous for
being at the service of any cause, good or bad. Here Socrates gently
reminds his audience of this charge and alludes to Agathon's method for
praising anyone (195A2).
51. Socrates here uses a pun; the word for "talk" is a homonym for
"lover" (*erōn*).

But I didn't even know the method for giving praise; and it was in ignorance that I agreed to take part in this. So "the tongue" promised, and "the mind" did not.[52] Goodbye to that! I'm not giving another eulogy using that method, not at all—I wouldn't be able to do it!—but, if you wish, I'd like to tell the truth my way. I want to avoid any comparison with your speeches, so as not to give you a reason to laugh at me. So look, Phaedrus, would a speech like this satisfy your requirement? You will hear the truth about Love, and the words and phrasing will take care of themselves."

199B

Then Aristodemus said that Phaedrus and the others urged him to speak in the way he thought was required, whatever it was.

"Well then, Phaedrus," said Socrates, "allow me to ask Agathon a few little questions, so that, once I have his agreement, I may speak on that basis."

199C

"You have my permission," said Phaedrus. "Ask away."

---

52. The allusion is to Euripides, *Hippolytus* 612.

SOCRATES[53]
QUESTIONS
AGATHON

AFTER THAT, said Aristodemus, Socrates began:[54]
"Indeed, Agathon, my friend, I thought you led the way beautifully into your speech when you said that one should first show the qualities of Love himself, and only then those of his deeds. I much admire that beginning. Come, then, since you have beautifully and magnificently expounded his qualities in other ways, tell me this, too, about Love. Is Love such as to be a love of something or of nothing? I'm not asking if he is born *of* some mother or father,[55] (for the question whether Love is love of mother or of father would really be ridiculous), but it's as if I'm asking this about a father—whether a father is the father *of* something or not. You'd tell me, of course, if you

199D

---

53. It is characteristic of Socrates as Plato represents him that, instead of giving a speech as his own, he first questions the previous speaker and then supplies a speech as coming from someone else. The views presented by Socrates, however, are generally held by scholars to be those of Plato and not those of the historical Socrates (see our Introduction, p. xii). But readers in search of Plato's own views should keep in mind that Plato is the author of all seven speeches.

54. In contrast with Agathon's, Socrates' style in these early questions is deliberately rough; the structure of his sentences is governed by the complex points he is trying to make.

55. Socrates puns here on "of" (expressed in Greek by the genitive case). He is treating love (*erōs*) here as a species of desire, which must be desire *of* something. It will follow that love is not symmetrical: if A loves or desires B, it does not follow that B loves or desires A. See above, p. 11, n. 16 (on Phaedrus' speech), and below, 205D.

40

wanted to give me a good answer,[56] that it's *of* a son or a daughter that a father is the father. Wouldn't you?"

"Certainly," said Agathon.

"Then does the same go for the mother?"

He agreed to that also.

199E

"Well, then," said Socrates, "answer a little more fully, and you will understand better what I want. If I should ask, "What about this: a brother, just insofar as he *is* a brother,[57] is he the brother of something or not?""

He said that he was.

"And he's of a brother or a sister, isn't he?"

He agreed.

"Now try to tell me about love," he said. "Is Love the love of nothing or of something?"

"Of something, surely!"

200A

"Then keep this object of love in mind, and remember what it is. But tell me this much: does Love desire that of which it is the love, or not?"

"Certainly," he said.

"At the time he desires and loves something, does he actually have what he desires and loves at that time, or doesn't he?"

"He doesn't. At least, that wouldn't be likely,"[58] he said.

"Instead of what's *likely*," said Socrates, "ask yourself whether it's *necessary* that this be so: a thing that desires desires something of which it is in need; otherwise, if it were not in need, it would not desire it. I can't tell you, Agathon, how strongly it strikes me that this is necessary. But how about you?"

200B

---

56. "A good answer": Here and elsewhere in questioning Agathon, Socrates uses forms of *kalos*, which in other contexts means "beautiful." Socrates chooses this term of commendation to suit Agathon's interest in the aesthetic qualities of love.

57. "Just insofar as he *is* a brother": literally, "that which a brother is." Such language usually refers to a Platonic Form. Here Socrates asks after what it is to be a brother; his point is that being a brother involves being the brother *of* another sibling.

58. The standard of what is likely (*to eikos*) was associated with Gorgias and his school of orators. See *Phaedrus* 267A.

"I think so too."

"Good. Now then, would someone who is tall, want to be tall? Or someone who is strong want to be strong?"

"Impossible, on the basis of what we've agreed."

"Presumably because no one is in need of those things he already has."

"True."

200C "But maybe a strong man could want to be strong," said Socrates, "or a fast one fast, or a healthy one healthy: in cases like these, you might think people really do want to be things they already are and do want to have qualities they already have—I bring them up so they won't deceive us. But in these cases, Agathon, if you stop to think about them, you will see that these people are what they are at the present time, whether they want to be or not, by a logical necessity.[59] And who, may I ask, would ever bother to desire what's necessary in any event? But when someone says 'I am healthy, but that's just what I want to be,' or 'I am rich, but that's just what I want to be,' or 'I desire the 200D very things that I have,' let us say to him: 'You already have riches and health and strength in your possession, my man; what you want is to possess these things in time to come, since in the present, whether you want to or not, you have them. Whenever you say, *I desire what I already have,* ask yourself whether you don't mean this: *I want the things I have now to be mine in the future as well.*' Wouldn't he agree?"

According to Aristodemus, Agathon said that he would.

So Socrates said, "Then this is what it is to love something which is not at hand, which the lover does not have: it is to desire the preservation of what he now has in time to come, so 200E that he will have it then."

"Quite so," he said.

"So such a man or anyone else who has a desire desires what

---

59. It is necessary, as a matter of logic, that a strong man is strong. What is not necessary, as Socrates will point out, is that a strong man *remain* strong.

is not at hand and not present, what he does not have, and what he is not, and that of which he is in need; for such are the objects of desire and love."

"Certainly," he said.

"Come, then," said Socrates. "Let us review the points on which we've agreed. Aren't they, first, that Love is the love of something, and, second, that he loves things of which he has a present need?"[60]

201A

"Yes," he said.

"Now, remember, in addition to these points, what you said in your speech about what it is that Love loves. If you like, I'll remind you. I think you said something like this: that the gods' quarrels were settled by love of beautiful things, for there is no love of ugly ones.[61] Didn't you say something like that?"

"I did," said Agathon.

"And that's a suitable thing to say, my friend," said Socrates. "But if this is so, wouldn't Love have to be a desire for beauty, and never for ugliness?"

He agreed.

201B

"And we also agreed that he loves just what he needs and does not have."

"Yes," he said.

"So Love needs beauty, then, and does not have it."

"Necessarily," he said.

"So! If something needs beauty and has got no beauty at all, would you still say that it is beautiful?"

"Certainly not."

"Then do you still agree that Love is beautiful, if those things are so?"

Then Agathon said, "It turns out, Socrates, I didn't know what I was talking about in that speech."

201C

"It was a beautiful speech, anyway, Agathon," said Socrates. "Now take it a little further. Don't you think that good things are always beautiful as well?"

---

60. The first point was agreed at 200A1, the second at 200E6.
61. 197B3−5.

"I do."

"Then if Love needs beautiful things, and if all good things are beautiful, he will need good things too."

"As for me, Socrates," he said, "I am unable to challenge you. Let it be as you say."

"Then it's the truth, my beloved Agathon, that you are unable to challenge," he said. "It is not hard at all to challenge Socrates."

DIOTIMA[62] QUESTIONS SOCRATES

N OW I'LL LET YOU GO. I shall try to go through for 201D
you the speech about Love I once heard from a woman of Mantinea, Diotima—a woman who was wise
about many things besides this: once she even put off the plague
for ten years by telling the Athenians what sacrifices to make.
She is the one who taught me the art of love, and I shall go
through her speech as best I can on my own, using what
Agathon and I have agreed to as a basis.

Following your lead, Agathon, one should first describe who
Love is and what he is like, and afterwards describe his
works. . . .[63]   201E

I think it will be easiest for me to proceed the way Diotima
did and tell you how she questioned me. You see, I had told her
almost the same things Agathon told me just now: that Love is a
great god and that he belongs to beautiful things.[64] And she
used the very same arguments against me that I used against
Agathon; she showed how, according to my very own speech,
Love is neither beautiful nor good.

So I said, "What do you mean, Diotima? Is Love ugly, then,
and bad?"

---

62. Diotima is apparently a fictional character contrived by Socrates for
this occasion. See the introduction and our notes on 202D4 and 205D10.
63. See Agathon's introduction at 195A, and Socrates' ironical allusion to
the method at 199A – B.
64. "That he belongs to beautiful things": The Greek is ambiguous between "Love loves beautiful things" (objective genitive) and "Love is
one of the beautiful things" (partitive genitive). Agathon had asserted
the former (197B5, 201A5), and this will be a premise in Diotima's argument, but he asserted the latter as well (195A7), and this is what Diotima proceeds to refute.

But she said, "Watch your tongue! Do you really think that, if
202A   a thing is not beautiful, it has to be ugly?"

"I certainly do."

"And if a thing's not wise, it's ignorant? Or haven't you found
out yet that there's something in between wisdom and
ignorance?"

"What's that?"

"It's judging things correctly without being able to give a
reason. Surely you see that this is not the same as knowing—for
how could knowledge be unreasoning? And it's not ignorance
either—for how could what hits the truth be ignorance? Correct
judgment, of course, has this character: it is *in between* understanding and ignorance."

202B   "True," said I, "as you say."

"Then don't force whatever is not beautiful to be ugly, or
whatever is not good to be bad. It's the same with Love: when
you agree he is neither good nor beautiful, you need not think
he is ugly and bad; he could be something in between," she said.

"Yet everyone agrees he's a great god," I said.

"Only those who don't know?" she said. "Is that how you
mean 'everyone'? Or do you include those who do know?"

"Oh, everyone together."

And she laughed. "Socrates, how could those who say that
202C   he's not a god at all agree that he's a great god?"

"Who says that?" I asked.

"You, for one," she said, "and I for another."

"How can you say this!" I exclaimed.

"That's easy," said she. "Tell me, wouldn't you say that all
gods are beautiful and happy?[65] Surely you'd never say a god is
not beautiful or happy?"

"Zeus! Not I," I said.

"Well, by calling anyone 'happy,' don't you mean they possess good and beautiful things?"

202D   "Certainly."

"What about Love? You agreed he needs good and beautiful
things, and that's why he desires them—because he needs
them."

---

65. Agathon had maintained this at 195A5.

"I certainly did."[66]

"Then how could he be a god if he has no share in good and beautiful things?"

"There's no way he could, apparently."

"Now do you see? You don't believe Love is a god either!"

"Then, what could Love be?" I asked. "A mortal?"

"Certainly not."

"Then, what is he?"

"He's like what we mentioned before," she said. "He is in between mortal and immortal."

"What do you mean, Diotima?"

"He's a great spirit, Socrates. Everything spiritual, you see, is *202E* in between god and mortal."[67]

"What is their function?" I asked.

"They are messengers who shuttle back and forth between the two, conveying prayer and sacrifice from men to gods, while to men they bring commands from the gods and gifts in return for sacrifices. Being in the middle of the two, they round out the whole and bind fast the all to all.[68] Through them all divination passes, through them the art of priests in sacrifice and ritual, in *203A* enchantment, prophecy, and sorcery. Gods do not mix with men; they mingle and converse with us through spirits instead, whether we are awake or asleep. He who is wise in any of these ways is a man of the spirit, but he who is wise in any other way, in a profession or any manual work, is merely a mechanic. These spirits are many and various, then, and one of them is Love."

"Who are his father and mother?" I asked.   *203B*

"That's rather a long story," she said. "I'll tell it to you, all the same."

---

66. Agathon agreed to this at 201AB.

67. The generic word for the spiritual, *daimonion*, is the same as that used for the spirit that is said to warn Socrates when he is about to do wrong (e.g., *Apology* 31C).

68. Cf. Aristophanes' speech, esp. 191D.

THE SPEECH OF
DIOTIMA

W HEN APHRODITE WAS BORN, the gods held a celebration. Poros,[69] the son of Metis, was there among them. When they had feasted, Penia[70] came begging, as poverty does when there's a party, and stayed by the gates. Now Poros got drunk on nectar (there was no wine yet, you see) and, feeling drowsy, went into the garden of Zeus, where he fell asleep. Then Penia schemed up a plan to relieve her lack of resources: she would get a child from Poros. So she lay beside him and got pregnant with Love. That is why Love was born to follow Aphrodite and serve her: because he was conceived on the day of her birth. And that's why he is also by nature a lover of beauty, because Aphrodite herself is especially beautiful.

203C

"As the son of Poros and Penia, his lot in life is set to be like theirs. In the first place, he is always poor, and he's far from being delicate and beautiful (as ordinary people think he is); instead, he is tough and shriveled and shoeless and homeless, always lying on the dirt without a bed, sleeping at people's doorsteps and in roadsides under the sky, having his mother's nature, always living with Need. But on his father's side he is a schemer after the beautiful and the good; he is brave, impetuous, and intense, an awesome hunter, always weaving snares, resourceful in his pursuit of intelligence, a lover of wisdom[71] through all his life, a genius with enchantments, potions, and clever pleadings.

203D

"He is by nature neither immortal nor mortal. But now he springs to life when he gets his way; now he dies—all in the very

203E

---

69. *Poros* means "way," "resource." His mother's name, *Mētis*, means "cunning."
70. "Poverty."
71. "Lover of wisdom" (*philosophōn*): one who pursues philosophy.

same day. Because he is his father's son, however, he keeps coming back to life, but then anything he finds his way to always slips away, and for this reason Love is never completely without resources, nor is he ever rich.

"He is in between wisdom and ignorance as well. In fact, you see, none of the gods loves wisdom or wants to become wise—for they are wise—and no one else who is wise already loves wisdom; on the other hand, no one who is ignorant will love wisdom either or want to become wise. For what's especially difficult about being ignorant is that you are content with yourself, even though you're neither beautiful and good nor intelligent. If you don't think you need anything, of course you won't want what you don't think you need." *204A*

"In that case, Diotima, who *are* the people who love wisdom, if they are neither wise nor ignorant?" *204B*

"That's obvious," she said. "A child could tell you. Those who love wisdom fall in between those two extremes. And Love is one of them, because he is in love with what is beautiful, and wisdom is extremely beautiful. It follows that Love *must* be a lover of wisdom and, as such, is in between being wise and being ignorant. This, too, comes to him from his parentage, from a father who is wise and resourceful and a mother who is not wise and lacks resource.

"My dear Socrates, that, then, is the nature of the Spirit called Love. Considering what you thought about Love, it's no surprise that you were led into thinking of Love as you did. On the basis of what you say, I conclude that you thought Love was *being loved*, rather than *being a lover*. I think that's why Love struck you as beautiful in every way: because it is what is really beautiful and graceful that deserves to be loved,[72] and this is perfect and highly blessed; but being a lover takes a different form, which I have just described." *204C*

So I said, "All right then, my friend. What you say about Love is beautiful, but if you're right, what use is Love to human beings?" *204D*

---

72. "What deserves to be loved": the argument turns on an ambiguity in the Greek between "being loved" and "lovable," both of which are involved in the sense of *eraston*.

"I'll try to teach you that, Socrates, after I finish this. So far I've been explaining the character and the parentage of Love. Now, according to you,[73] he is love for beautiful things. But suppose someone asks us, 'Socrates and Diotima, what is the point of loving beautiful things?'

"It's clearer this way: 'The lover of beautiful things has a desire; what does he desire?'"

"That they become his own," I said.

"But that answer calls for still another question, that is, 'What will this man have, when the beautiful things he wants have become his own?'"

204E I said there was no way I could give a ready answer to that question.

Then she said, "Suppose someone changes the question, putting 'good' in place of 'beautiful,' and asks you this: 'Tell me, Socrates, a lover of good things has a desire; what does he desire?'"

"That they become his own," I said.

"And what will he have, when the good things he wants have become his own?"

"This time it's easier to come up with the answer," I said.
205A "He'll have happiness."[74]

"That's what makes happy people happy, isn't it—possessing good things. There's no need to ask further, 'What's the point of wanting happiness?' The answer you gave seems to be final."

"True," I said.

"Now this desire for happiness, this kind of love—do you think it is common to all human beings and that everyone wants to have good things forever and ever? What would you say?"

"Just that," I said. "It is common to all."

"Then, Socrates, why don't we say that everyone is in love,"
205B she asked, "since everyone always loves the same things? In-

---

73. See 202D.
74. Happiness: *eudaimonia*. No English word catches the full range of this term, which is used for the whole of well-being and the good life.

stead, we say some people are in love and others not; why is that?"

"I wonder about that myself," I said.

"It's nothing to wonder about," she said. "It's because we divide out a special kind of love, and we refer to it by the word that means the whole—'love'; and for the other kinds of love we use other words."

"What do you mean?" I asked.

"Well, you know, for example, that 'poetry' has a very wide range, when it is used to mean 'creativity.'[75] After all, everything that is responsible for creating something out of nothing is a kind of poetry; and so all the creations of every craft and profession are themselves a kind of poetry, and everyone who practices a craft is a poet." *205C*

"True."

"Nevertheless," she said, "as you also know, these craftsmen are not called poets. We have other words for them, and out of the whole of poetry we have marked off one part, the part the Muses give us with melody and rhythm, and we refer to this by the word that means the whole. For this alone is called 'poetry,' and those who practice this part of poetry are called poets."

"True." *205D*

"That's also how it is with love. The main point is this: every desire for good things or for happiness is 'the supreme and treacherous love'[76] in everyone. But those who pursue this along any of its many other ways—through making money, or through the love of sports, or through philosophy—we don't say that *these* people are in love, and we don't call them lovers. It's only when people are devoted exclusively to one special kind of love that we use these words that really belong to the whole of it: 'love' and 'in love' and 'lovers.'"

---

75. "Poetry" translates *poiēsis,* which means any kind of production or creation. Greeks used the word *poiētēs,* however, mainly for poets—for writers of metrical verses that were actually set to music.
76. This appears to be a tag line of poetry, as the language is poetic. The source is unknown.

"I am beginning to see your point," I said.

"Now there is a certain story," she said, "according to which
205E   lovers are those people who seek their other halves.[77] But according to my story, a lover does not seek the half or the whole,
unless, my friend, it turns out to be good as well. I say this
because people are even willing to cut off their own arms and
legs if they think they are diseased. I don't think an individual
takes joy in what belongs to him personally unless by 'belonging
to me' he means 'good' and by 'belonging to another' he means
'bad.' That's because what everyone loves is really nothing other
206A   than the good. Do you disagree?"

"Zeus! Not I," I said.

"Now, then," she said. "Can we simply say that people love
the good?"

"Yes," I said.

"But shouldn't we add that, in loving it, they want the good
to be theirs?"

"We should."

"And not only that," she said. "They want the good to be
theirs forever, don't they?"

"We should add that too."

"In a word, then, love is wanting to possess the good
forever."
206B   "That's very true," I said.

"This, then, is the object of love,"[78] she said. "In view of that,
how do people pursue it if they are truly in love? What do they
do with the eagerness and zeal we call love? What is the real
purpose of love? Can you say?"

"If I could," I said, "I wouldn't be your student, filled with
admiration for your wisdom, and trying to learn these very
things."

---

77. This was the point of Aristophanes' speech. Diotima's reference to
that speech makes it hard to believe that Socrates is reporting a conversation he actually had with a woman named Diotima and lends cre-
dence to the hypothesis that Diotima is a character Socrates dreamed up
for this occasion.

78. "The object of love": here we translate Bast's emendation from τοῦτο
in the mss to τούτου. In this we follow Bury; cf. Vlastos ("The Individual as Object of Love in Plato," p. 21, n. 57).

"Well, I'll tell you," she said. "It is giving birth in beauty,[79] whether in body or in soul."

"It would take divination to figure out what you mean. I can't."

"Well, I'll tell you more clearly," she said. "All of us are pregnant, Socrates, both in body and in soul, and, as soon as we come to a certain age, we naturally desire to give birth. Now no one can possibly give birth in anything ugly; only in something beautiful. That's because when a man and a woman come together in order to give birth, this is a godly affair. Pregnancy, reproduction—this is an immortal thing for a mortal animal to do, and it cannot occur in anything that is out of harmony, but ugliness is out of harmony with all that is godly. Beauty, however, is in harmony with the divine. Therefore the goddess who presides at childbirth—she's called Moira or Eileithuia—is really Beauty.[80] That's why, whenever pregnant animals or persons draw near to beauty, they become gentle and joyfully disposed and give birth and reproduce; but near ugliness they are foul-faced and draw back in pain; they turn away and shrink back and do not reproduce, and because they hold on to what they carry inside them, the labor is painful. This is the source of the great excitement about beauty that comes to anyone who is pregnant and already teeming with life: beauty releases them from their great pain. You see, Socrates," she said, "what Love wants is not beauty, as you think it is."[81]

"Well, what is it, then?"

"Reproduction and birth in beauty."

206C

206D

206E

---

79. "Birth in beauty" (*tokos en kalōi*): The preposition Diotima uses is ambiguous between "in" and "in the presence of." She may mean that the pregnant person causes the newborn (which may be an idea) to be within a beautiful person; or she may mean that the pregnant person simply is stimulated to give birth in the presence of a beautiful person. (On Aristophanes' more comic use of the notion of Interior Reproduction, see 191C.)

80. Moira or Eileithuia: Moira, whose name means "the Dispenser" as Bury translates it, is known mainly as a Fate, but she is also a birth goddess in Homer (*Iliad*, xxiv.209). The identification with the birth goddess Eileithuia is made in Pindar (*Olympian Odes* vi.41, *Nemean Odes* vii.1).

81. See 201E, 204D3.

"Maybe," I said.

"Certainly," she said. "Now, why reproduction? It's because reproduction goes on forever; it is what mortals have in place of immortality. A lover must desire immortality along with the good, if what we agreed earlier was right, that Love wants to possess the good forever.[82] It follows from our argument that Love must desire immortality."

207A

All this she taught me, on those occasions when she spoke on the art of love.[83] And once she asked, "What do you think causes love and desire, Socrates? Don't you see what an awful state a wild animal is in when it wants to reproduce? Footed and winged animals alike, all are plagued by the disease of Love. First they are sick for intercourse with each other, then for nurturing their young—for their sake the weakest animals stand ready to do battle against the strongest and even to die for them, and they may be racked with famine in order to feed their young. They would do anything for their sake. Human beings, you'd think, would do this because they understand the reason for it; but what causes wild animals to be in such a state of love? Can you say?"

207B

207C

And I said again that I didn't know.

So she said, "How do you think you'll ever master the art of love, if you don't know that?"

"But that's why I came to you, Diotima, as I just said. I knew I needed a teacher. So tell me what causes this, and everything else that belongs to the art of love."

"If you really believe that Love by its nature aims at what we have often agreed it does, then don't be surprised at the answer," she said. "For among animals the principle is the same as with us, and mortal nature seeks so far as possible to live forever and be immortal. And this is possible in one way only: by reproduction, because it always leaves behind a new young one in place of the old. Even while each living thing is said to be alive and to be the same—as a person is said to be the same from childhood till

207D

---

82. 206A9–13.
83. "The art of love": *ta erōtika*. See 177D8, with our note on the expression.

he turns into an old man—even then he never consists of the same things, though he is called the same, but he is always being renewed and in other respects passing away, in his hair and flesh and bones and blood and his entire body. And it's not just in his *207E* body, but in his soul too, for none of his manners, customs, opinions, desires, pleasures, pains, or fears ever remains the same, but some are coming to be in him while others are passing away. And what is still far stranger than that is that not only does one branch of knowledge come to be in us while another passes away and that we are never the same even in respect of *208A* our knowledge, but that each single piece of knowledge has the same fate. For what we call *studying* exists because knowledge is leaving us, because forgetting is the departure of knowledge, while studying puts back a fresh memory in place of what went away, thereby preserving a piece of knowledge, so that it seems to be the same. And in that way everything mortal is preserved, not, like the divine, by always being the same in every way, but *208B* because what is departing and aging leaves behind something new, something such as it had been. By this device, Socrates," she said, "what is mortal shares in immortality, whether it is a body or anything else, while the immortal has another way. So don't be surprised if everything naturally values its own off-spring, because it is for the sake of immortality that everything shows this zeal, which is Love."

Yet when I heard her speech I was amazed, and spoke: "Well," said I, "Most wise Diotima, is this really the way it is?" *208C*

And in the manner of a perfect sophist she said, "Be sure of it, Socrates. Look, if you will, at how human beings seek honor. You'd be amazed at their irrationality, if you didn't have in mind what I spoke about and if you hadn't pondered the awful state of love they're in, wanting to become famous and 'to lay up glory immortal forever,'[84] and how they're ready to brave any danger for the sake of this, much more than they are for their children; and they are prepared to spend money, suffer through all sorts of ordeals, and even die for the sake of glory. Do you really think *208D* that Alcestis would have died for Admetus," she asked, "or that Achilles would have died after Patroclus, or that your Kodros

---

84. A line of poetry of unknown origin.

would have died so as to preserve the throne for his sons,[85] if they hadn't expected the memory of their virtue—which we still hold in honor—to be immortal?[86] Far from it," she said. "I believe that anyone will do anything for the sake of immortal virtue and the glorious fame that follows; and the better the people, the more they will do, for they are all in love with immortality.

208E

"Now, some people are pregnant in body, and for this reason turn more to women and pursue love in that way, providing themselves through childbirth with immortality and remembrance and happiness, as they think, for all time to come; while others are pregnant in soul—because there surely *are* those who are even more pregnant in their souls than in their bodies, and these are pregnant with what is fitting for a soul to bear and bring to birth. And what is fitting? Wisdom and the rest of virtue, which all poets beget, as well as all the craftsmen who are said to be creative. But by far the greatest and most beautiful part of wisdom deals with the proper ordering of cities and households, and that is called moderation and justice.[87] When someone has been pregnant with these in his soul from early youth, while he is still a virgin, and, having arrived at the proper age, desires to beget and give birth, he too will certainly go about seeking the beauty in which he would beget; for he will never beget in anything ugly. Since he is pregnant, then, he is much more drawn to bodies that are beautiful than to those that are ugly; and if he also has the luck to find a soul that is beautiful and noble and well-formed, he is even more drawn to this combination; such a man makes him instantly teem with ideas and arguments[88] about virtue—the qualities a virtuous man should have and the customary activities in which he should

209A

209B

209C

---

85. Kodros was the legendary last king of Athens. He gave his life to satisfy a prophecy that promised victory to Athens and salvation from the invading Dorians if their king was killed by the enemy.
86. Compare Diotima's account of self-sacrifice with Phaedrus' speech at 179B ff, where the love in question is more personal.
87. The allusion here is to the art of politics as it is described in the conversation between Protagoras and Socrates in the *Protagoras*.
88. "Ideas and arguments": *logoi*. *Logos* has more meanings than can be captured by any single English word.

engage; and so he tries to educate him. In my view, you see, when he makes contact with someone beautiful and keeps company with him, he conceives and gives birth to what he has been carrying inside him for ages. And whether they are together or apart, he remembers that beauty. And in common with him he nurtures the newborn; such people, therefore, have much more to share than do the parents of human children, and have a firmer bond of friendship, because the children in whom they have a share are more beautiful and more immortal. Everyone would rather have such children than human ones, and would look up to Homer, Hesiod, and the other good poets with envy and admiration for the offspring they have left behind— offspring, which, because they are immortal themselves, provide their parents with immortal glory and remembrance. For example," she said, "those are the sort of children Lycourgos[89] left behind in Sparta as the saviors of Sparta and virtually all of Greece. Among you the honor goes to Solon for his creation of your laws. Other men in other places everywhere, Greek or barbarian, have brought a host of beautiful deeds into the light and begotten every kind of virtue. Already many shrines have sprung up to honor them for their immortal children, which hasn't happened yet to anyone for human offspring.

209D

209E

"Even you, Socrates, could probably come to be initiated into these rites of love. But as for the purpose of these rites when they are done correctly—that is the final and highest mystery, and I don't know if you are capable of it. I myself will tell you," she said, "and I won't stint any effort. And you must try to follow if you can.

210A

"A lover who goes about this matter correctly must begin in his youth to devote himself to beautiful bodies. First, if the leader[90] leads aright, he should love one body and beget beautiful ideas there; then he should realize that the beauty of any one body is brother to the beauty of any other and that if he is to pursue beauty of form he'd be very foolish not to think that the

210B

89. Lycourgos was supposed to have been the founder of the oligarchic laws and stern customs of Lacedaimon (Sparta). Socrates' admiration for these cannot have been popular in democratic Athens.
90. The leader: Love.

beauty of all bodies is one and the same. When he grasps this, he must become a lover of all beautiful bodies, and he must think that this wild gaping after just one body is a small thing and despise it.

"After this he must think that the beauty of people's souls is more valuable than the beauty of their bodies, so that if someone is decent in his soul, even though he is scarcely blooming in his 210C body, our lover must be content to love and care for him and to seek to give birth to such ideas as will make young men better. The result is that our lover will be forced to gaze at the beauty of activities and laws and to see that all this is akin to itself, with the result that he will think that the beauty of bodies is a thing of no importance. After customs he must move on to various kinds of knowledge. The result is that he will see the beauty of knowl- 210D edge and be looking mainly not at beauty in a single example— as a servant would who favored the beauty of a little boy or a man or a single custom (being a slave, of course, he's low and small-minded)—but the lover is turned to the great sea of beauty, and, gazing upon this, he gives birth to many gloriously beautiful ideas and theories, in unstinting love of wisdom,[91] un- 210E til, having grown and been strengthened there, he catches sight of such knowledge, and it is the knowlege of such beauty . . .

"Try to pay attention to me," she said, "as best you can. You see, the man who has been thus far guided in matters of Love, who has beheld beautiful things in the right order and correctly, is coming now to the goal of Loving: all of a sudden he will catch sight of something wonderfully beautiful in its nature; that, Soc- 211A rates, is the reason for all his earlier labors:

"First, it always *is* and neither comes to be nor passes away, neither waxes nor wanes. Second, it is not beautiful this way and ugly that way, nor beautiful at one time and ugly at another, nor beautiful in relation to one thing and ugly in relation to another; nor is it beautiful here but ugly there, as it would be if it were beautiful for some people and ugly for others.[92] Nor will the

---

91. "Love of wisdom": *philosophia*.

92. "As it would be if it were beautiful for some people and ugly for others": Bury rejects this as an inept gloss, following Voegelin. It is accepted, however, by Burnet, Dover, and most other editors.

beautiful appear to him in the guise of a face or hands or anything else that belongs to the body. It will not appear to him as
one idea or one kind of knowledge. It is not anywhere in another
thing, as in an animal, or in earth, or in heaven, or in anything   *211B*
else, but itself by itself with itself, it is always one in form; and all
the other beautiful things share in that, in such a way that when
those others come to be or pass away, this does not become the
least bit smaller or greater nor suffer any change. So when someone rises by these stages, through loving boys correctly, and
begins to see this beauty, he has almost grasped his goal. This is
what it is to go aright, or be lead by another, into the mystery of   *211C*
Love: one goes always upwards for the sake of this Beauty, start-
ing out from beautiful things and using them like rising stairs:
from one body to two and from two to all beautiful bodies, then
from beautiful bodies to beautiful customs, and from customs to
learning beautiful things, and from these lessons he arrives[93] in
the end at this lesson, which is learning of this very Beauty, so
that in the end he comes to know just what it is to be beautiful.   *211D*

"And there in life, Socrates, my friend," said the woman from
Mantinea, "there if anywhere should a person live his life, be-
holding that Beauty. If you once see that, it won't occur to you
to measure beauty by gold or clothing or beautiful boys and
youths—who, if you see them now, strike you out of your
senses, and make you, you and many others, eager to be with
the boys you love and look at them forever, if there were any
way to do that, forgetting food and drink, everything but looking
at them and being with them. But how would it be, in our view,"
she said, "if someone got to see the Beautiful itself, absolute,   *211E*
pure, unmixed, not polluted by human flesh or colors or any
other great nonsense of mortality, but if he could see the divine
Beauty itself in its one form? Do you think it would be a poor life   *212A*
for a human being to look there and to behold it by that which
he ought,[94] and to be with it? Or haven't you remembered," she
said, "that in that life alone, when he looks at Beauty in the only

---

93. Here we follow the manuscripts, rejecting Usener's emendation.
The finite verb form of the manuscripts is more vivid.
94. ". . . which he ought": apparently, by the mind's eye.

way that Beauty can be seen—only then will it become possible
for him to give birth not to images of virtue (because he's in
touch with no images), but to true virtue (because he is in touch
with the true Beauty). The love of the gods belongs to anyone
who has given birth to true virtue and nourished it, and if any
212B   human being could become immortal, it would be he."

This, Phaedrus and the rest of you, was what Diotima told
me. I was persuaded. And once persuaded, I try to persuade
others too that human nature can find no better workmate for
acquiring this than Love. That's why I say that every man must
honor Love, why I honor the rites of Love myself and practice
them with special diligence, and why I commend them to others.
Now and always I praise the power and courage of Love so far as
212C   I am able. Consider this speech, then, Phaedrus, if you wish, a
speech in praise of Love. Or if not, call it whatever and however
you please to call it.

ALCIBIADES'
ENTRANCE

SOCRATES' SPEECH finished to loud applause. Meanwhile, Aristophanes was trying to make himself heard over their cheers in order to make a response to something Socrates had said about his own speech.[95] Then, all of a sudden, there was even more noise. A large drunken party had arrived at the courtyard door and they were rattling it loudly, accompanied by the shrieks of some flute-girl they had brought along. Agathon at that point called to his slaves:

"Go see who it is. If it's people we know, invite them in. If not, tell them the party's over, and we're about to turn in."

212D

A moment later they heard Alcibiades shouting in the courtyard, very drunk and very loud. He wanted to know where Agathon was, he demanded to see Agathon at once. Actually, he was half-carried into the house by the flute-girl and by some other companions of his, but, at the door, he managed to stand by himself, crowned with a beautiful wreath of violets and ivy and ribbons in his hair.

212E

"Good evening, gentlemen. I'm plastered," he announced. "May I join your party? Or should I crown Agathon with this wreath—which is all I came to do, anyway—and make myself scarce? I really couldn't make it yesterday," he continued, "but nothing could stop me tonight! See, I'm wearing the garland myself. I want this crown to come directly from my head to the head that belongs, I don't mind saying, to the cleverest and best looking man in town. Ah, you laugh; you think I'm drunk! Fine, go ahead—I know I'm right anyway. Well, what do you say? May I join you on these terms? Will you have a drink with me or not?"

213A

Naturally they all made a big fuss. They implored him to join

---

95. Cf. 204D–E.

them, they begged him to take a seat, and Agathon called him to his side. So Alcibiades, again with the help of his friends, approached Agathon. At the same time, he kept trying to take his ribbons off so that he could crown Agathon with them, but all he succeeded in doing was to push them further down his head until they finally slipped over his eyes. What with the ivy and all, he didn't see Socrates, who had made room for him on the couch as soon as he saw him. So Alcibiades sat down between Socrates and Agathon and, as soon as he did so, he put his arms around Agathon, kissed him, and placed the ribbons on his head.

213B

Agathon asked his slaves to take Alcibiades' sandals off. "We can all three fit on my couch," he said.

"What a good idea!" Alcibiades replied. "But wait a moment! Who's the third?"

As he said this, he turned around, and it was only then that he saw Socrates. No sooner had he seen him than he leaped up and cried:

213C

"Good lord, what's going on here? It's Socrates! You've trapped me again! You always do this to me—all of a sudden you'll turn up out of nowhere where I least expect you! Well, what do you want now? Why did you choose this particular couch? Why aren't you with Aristophanes or anyone else we could tease you about?[96] But no, you figured out a way to find a place next to the most handsome man in the room!"

"I beg you, Agathon," Socrates said, "protect me from this man! You can't imagine what it's like to be in love with him: from the very first moment he realized how I felt about him, he hasn't allowed me to say two words to anybody else—what am I saying, I can't so much as look at an attractive man but he flies into a fit of jealous rage. He yells; he threatens; he can hardly keep from slapping me around! Please, try to keep him under control. Could you perhaps make him forgive me? And if you can't, if he gets violent, will you defend me? The fierceness of his passion terrifies me!"

213D

---

96. "Anyone else we could tease you about": literally, "anyone else who is willingly an object of fun."

"I shall never forgive you!" Alcibiades cried. "I promise you, you'll pay for this! But for the moment," he said, turning to Agathon, "give me some of these ribbons. I'd better make a wreath for him as well—look at that magnificent head! Otherwise, I know, he'll make a scene. He'll be grumbling that, though I crowned you for your first victory, I didn't honor him even though he has never lost an argument in his life." *213E*

So Alcibiades took the ribbons, arranged them on Socrates' head, and lay back on the couch. Immediately, however, he started up again:

"Friends, you look sober to me; we can't have that! Let's have a drink! Remember our agreement? We need a master of ceremonies; who should it be? . . . Well, at least till you are all too drunk to care, I elect . . . myself! Who else? Agathon, I want the largest cup around . . . No! Wait! You! Bring me that cooling jar over there!" *214A*

He'd seen the cooling jar, and he realized it could hold more than two quarts of wine. He had the slaves fill it to the brim, drained it, and ordered them to fill it up again for Socrates.

"Not that the trick will have any effect on *him*," he told the group. "Socrates will drink whatever you put in front of him, but no one yet has seen him drunk."

The slave filled the jar and, while Socrates was drinking, Eryximachus said to Alcibiades:

"This is certainly most improper. We cannot simply pour the wine down our throats in silence: we must have some conversation, or at least a song. What we are doing now is hardly civilized." *214B*

What Alcibiades said to him was this:

"O Eryximachus, best possible son to the best possible, the most temperate father: Hi!"

"Greetings to you, too," Eryximachus replied. "Now what do you suggest we do?"

"Whatever you say. Ours to obey you, 'For a medical mind is worth a million others.'[97] Please prescribe what you think fit."

"Listen to me," Eryximachus said. "Earlier this evening we decided to use this occasion to offer a series of encomia of Love. *214C*

---

97. *Iliad* xi.514.

We all took our turn—in good order, from left to right—and gave our speeches, each according to his ability. You are the only one not to have spoken yet, though, if I may say so, you have certainly drunk your share. It's only proper, therefore, that you take your turn now. After you have spoken, you can decide on a topic for Socrates on your right; he can then do the same for the man to his right, and we can go around the table once again."

"Well said, O Eryximachus," Alcibiades replied. "But do you really think it's fair to put my drunken ramblings next to your sober orations? And anyway, my dear fellow, I hope you didn't believe a single word Socrates said: the truth is just the opposite! He's the one who will most surely beat me up if I dare praise anyone else in his presence—even a god!"

214D

"Hold your tongue!" Socrates said.[98]

"By god, don't you dare deny it!" Alcibiades shouted. "I would never—*never*—praise anyone else with you around."

"Well, why not just do that, if you want?" Eryximachus suggested. "Why don't you offer an encomium to Socrates?"

214E

"What do you mean?" asked Alcibiades. "Do you really think so, Eryximachus? Should I unleash myself upon him? Should I give him his punishment in front of all of you?"

"Now, wait a minute," Socrates said. "What do you have in mind? Are you going to praise me only in order to mock me? Is that it?"

"I'll only tell the truth—please, let me!"

"I would certainly like to hear the truth from you. By all means, go ahead," Socrates replied.

"Nothing can stop me now," said Alcibiades. "But here's what you can do: if I say anything that's not true, you can just interrupt, if you want, and correct me; at worst, there'll be mistakes in my speech, not lies. But you can't hold it against me if I don't get everything in the right order—I'll say things as they come to mind. And even a sober and unclouded mind would find it hard to come to terms with your bizarreness!"

215A

---

98. If Socrates truly put himself above the gods in this way he would be guilty of the grossest impiety; it is this suggestion that Socrates here tries to silence.

THE SPEECH OF
ALCIBIADES[99]

I'LL TRY TO PRAISE SOCRATES, my friends, but I'll have to use an image. And though he may think I'm trying to make fun of him, I assure you my image is no joke: it aims at the truth. Look at him! Isn't he just like a statue of Silenus? You know the kind of statue I mean; you'll find them in any shop in town. It's a Silenus sitting, his flute[100] or his pipes in his hands, and it's hollow. It's split right down the middle, and inside it's full of tiny statues of the gods. Now look at him again! Isn't he also just like the satyr Marsyas?[101]

215B

---

99. Alcibiades (c 450−404 B.C.) was a wealthy aristocrat of Athens, famous for his good looks. Orphaned at an early age, he was brought up as a ward of Pericles. He was the most celebrated of the young men who studied with Socrates and one whose subsequent career seemed to support the charge that Socrates had corrupted the youth (so Xenophon in the *Memorabilia* I.ii.12−16; see *Apology* 33AB and *Republic* VI 494B ff). The attachment of Socrates and Alcibiades was well known and is played upon at the opening of the *Protagoras*, 309A. Alcibiades had a meteoric career in politics. A brilliant politician and general, he led the Athenians into the Sicilian expedition of 415 B.C. but was barred from taking part in it owing to the charge that he had mutilated religious statues. Afterwards he aided the Spartans in their war against Athens. On his career, see especially Thucydides, V−VIII.
100. Flute: *aulos*. This is the conventional translation of the word, but the *aulos* was in fact a reed instrument and not a flute. It was held by the ancients to be the instrument that most strongly arouses the emotions.
101. Satyrs had the sexual appetites and manners of wild beasts and were usually portrayed with large erections. Sometimes they had horses' tails or ears, sometimes the traits of goats. Classical tradition did not clearly distinguish between a satyr and a silenus. Marsyas, in myth, was a satyr who dared compete in music with Apollo and was skinned alive for his impudence. For Socrates' resemblance to a satyr, see Xenophon, *Symposium* iv.19.

Nobody, not even you, Socrates, can deny that you *look* like them. But the resemblance goes beyond appearance, as you're about to hear.

You are impudent, contemptuous, and vile![102] No? If you won't admit it, I'll bring witnesses. And you're quite a flute-player, aren't you? In fact, you're much more marvelous than
215C   Marsyas, who needed instruments to cast his spells on people. And so does anyone who plays his tunes today—for even the tunes Olympos[103] played are Marsyas' work, since Olympos learned everything from him. Whether they are played by the greatest flautist or the meanest flute-girl, his melodies have in themselves the power to possess and so reveal those people who are ready for the god and his mysteries.[104] That's because his melodies are themselves divine. The only difference between you and Marsyas is that you need no instruments; you do exactly
215D   what he does, but with words alone. You know, people hardly ever take a speaker seriously, even if he's the greatest orator; but let anyone—man, woman, or child—listen to you or even to a poor account of what you say—and we are all transported, completely possessed.

Vulnerability - Admission of Control Socrates Holds over him

If I were to describe for you what an extraordinary effect his words have always had on me (I can feel it this moment even as
215E   I'm speaking), you might actually suspect that I'm drunk! Still, I swear to you, the moment he starts to speak, I am beside myself: my heart starts leaping in my chest, the tears come streaming

---

102. "Vile": *hubristēs*. In sexual contexts the word would normally be used of one who sexually abuses another, but Alcibiades here accuses Socrates of a different sort of abuse, as at 222A, where the point is that Socrates has mocked at Alcibiades' beauty. Agathon used the same word in calling attention to the mockery implied by Socrates' outrageously inflated praise at 175E7: in our translation, "now you've gone too far."
103. Olympos was a legendary musician who was said to be loved by Marsyas (*Minos* 318B5) and to have made music that moved its listeners out of their senses and so brought about a *katharsis* (*Ion* 533B, *Laws* 677D, and Aristotle's *Politics* 1340A8–12.)
104. This passage has been imitated at *Minos* 318B.

down my face, even the frenzied Corybantes[105] seem sane compared to me—and, let me tell you, I am not alone. I have heard Pericles and many other great orators, and I have admired their speeches. But nothing like this ever happened to me: they never upset me so deeply that my very own soul started protesting that my life—*my* life!—was no better than the most miserable slave's. And yet that is exactly how this Marsyas here at my side makes me feel all the time: he makes it seem that my life isn't worth living! You can't say that isn't true, Socrates. I know very well that you could make me feel that way this very moment if I gave you half a chance. He always traps me, you see, and he makes me admit that my political career is a waste of time, while all that matters is just what I most neglect: my personal shortcomings, which cry out for the closest attention. So I refuse to listen to him; I stop my ears and tear myself away from him, for, like the Sirens, he could make me stay by his side till I die.

216A

216B

Socrates is the only man in the world who has made me feel shame—ah, you didn't think I had it in me, did you? Yes, he makes me feel ashamed: I know perfectly well that I can't prove he's wrong when he tells me what I should do; yet, the moment I leave his side, I go back to my old ways: I cave in to my desire to please the crowd. My whole life has become one constant effort to escape from him and keep away, but when I see him, I feel deeply ashamed, because I'm doing nothing about my way of life, though I have already agreed with him that I should. Sometimes, believe me, I think I would be happier if he were dead. And yet I know that if he dies I'll be even more miserable. I can't live with him, and I can't live without him! What *can* I do about him?

{ conscience

216C

That's the effect of this satyr's music—on me and many others. But that's the least of it. He's like these creatures in all sorts of other ways; his powers are really extraordinary. Let me tell you about them, because, you can be sure of it, none of you really understands him. But, now I've started, I'm going to show you what he really is.

216D

---

105. Corybantes: legendary worshippers of Cybele, who brought about their own derangement through music and dance. See Plato's *Ion* 553E and *Laws* 790E.

To begin with, he's crazy about beautiful boys; he constantly follows them around in a perpetual daze. Also, he likes to say he's ignorant and knows nothing. Isn't this just like Silenus? Of course it is! And all this is just on the surface, like the outsides of those statues of Silenus. I wonder, my fellow drinkers, if you have any idea what a sober and temperate man he proves to be once you have looked inside. Believe me, it couldn't matter less to him whether a boy is beautiful. You can't imagine how little he cares whether a person is beautiful, or rich, or famous in any other way that most people admire. He considers all these possessions beneath contempt, and that's exactly how he considers all of us as well.[106] In public, I tell you, his whole life is one big game—a game of irony. I don't know if any of you have seen him when he's really serious. But I once caught him when he was open like Silenus' statues, and I had a glimpse of the figures he keeps hidden within: they were so godlike—so bright and beautiful, so utterly amazing—that I no longer had a choice—I just had to do whatever he told me.

216E

217A

What I thought at the time was that what he really wanted was *me*, and that seemed to me the luckiest coincidence: all I had to do was to let him have his way with me, and he would teach me everything he knew—believe me, I had a lot of confidence in my looks. Naturally, up to that time we'd never been alone together; one of my attendants had always been present. But with this in mind, I sent the attendant away, and met Socrates alone. (You see, in this company I must tell the whole truth: so pay attention. And, Socrates, if I say anything untrue, I want you to correct me.)

217B

So there I was, my friends, alone with him at last. My idea, naturally, was that he'd take advantage of the opportunity to tell me whatever it is that lovers say when they find themselves alone; I relished the moment. But no such luck! Nothing of the sort occurred. Socrates had his usual sort of conversation with me, and at the end of the day he went off.

217C

My next idea was to invite him to the gymnasium with me. We took exercise together, and I was sure that this would lead to

---

106. Probably Alcibiades intends his audience to understand "us beautiful boys" here.

something. He took exercise and wrestled with me many times when no one else was present. What can I tell you? I got nowhere. When I realized that my ploy had failed, I decided on a frontal attack. I refused to retreat from a battle I myself had begun, and I needed to know just where matters stood. So what I did was to invite him to dinner, as if *I* were his lover and he my young prey! To tell the truth, it took him quite a while to accept my invitation, but one day he finally arrived. That first time he *217D* left right after dinner: I was too shy to try to stop him. But on my next attempt, I started some discussion just as we were finishing our meal and kept him talking late into the night. When he said he should be going, I used the lateness of the hour as an excuse and managed to persuade him to spend the night at my house. He had had his meal on the couch next to mine, so he just made himself comfortable and lay down on it. No one else was there. *217E*

Now you must admit that my story so far has been perfectly decent; I could have told it in any company. But you'd never have heard me tell the rest of it, as you're about to do, if it weren't that, as the saying goes, 'there's truth in wine when the slaves have left'—and when they're present, too.[107] Also, would it be fair to Socrates for me to praise him and yet to fail to reveal one of his proudest accomplishments? And, furthermore, you know what people say about snakebite—that you'll only talk about it with your fellow victims: only they will understand the pain and for- *218A* give you for all the things it made you do. Well, something much more painful than a snake has bitten me in my most sensitive part—I mean my heart, or my soul, or whatever you want to call it, which has been struck and bitten by philosophy, whose grip on young and eager souls is much more vicious than a viper's and makes them do the most amazing things. Now, all you peo- ple here, Phaedrus, Agathon, Eryximachus, Pausanias, Aristode- *218B* mus, Aristophanes—I need not mention Socrates himself—and

---

107. The Greek word for children, *paides*, also means slaves. The origi- nal proverb ran, "There's truth in wine and children"; Alcibiades plays on an apparently well-known pun on the proverb: "There's truth in wine without slaves" (that is, drinkers speak freely when slaves are absent). He then adds that, to a man in his drunken condition, the pre- sence of slaves makes no difference. Slaves *are* present as he speaks (218B5). See Dover's note on the passage.

all the rest, have all shared in the madness, the Bacchic frenzy of philosophy. And that's why you will hear the rest of my story; you will understand and forgive both what I did then and what I say now. As for the house slaves and for anyone else who is not an initiate, my story's not for you: block your ears!

218C   To get back to the story. The lights were out; the slaves had left; the time was right, I thought, to come to the point and tell him freely what I had in mind. So I shook him and whispered:

"Socrates, are you asleep?"

"No, no, not at all," he replied.

"You know what I've been thinking?"

"Well, no, not really."

"I think," I said, "you're the only worthy lover I have ever had—and yet, look how shy you are with me! Well, here's how I look at it. It would be really stupid not to give you anything you
218D   want: you can have me, my belongings, anything my friends might have.[108] Nothing is more important to me than becoming the best man I can be, and no one can help me more than you to reach that aim. With a man like you, in fact, I'd be much more ashamed of what wise people would say if I did *not* take you as my lover, than I would of what all the others, in their foolishness, would say if I did."

He heard me out, and then he said in that absolutely inimitable ironic manner of his:

218E   "Dear Alcibiades, if you are right in what you say about me, you are already more accomplished than you think. If I really have in me the power to make you a better man, then you can see in me a beauty that is really beyond description and makes your own remarkable good looks pale in comparison. But, then, is this a fair exchange that you propose? You seem to me to want more than your proper share: you offer me the merest appearance of beauty, and in return you want the thing itself, 'gold
219A   in exchange for bronze.'[109]

---

108. For a sense of how much it was appropriate for a lover to give up for his love, see 183A4−B2. For a description of a young man's eagerness to acquire wisdom from a Sophist, see *Protagoras* 310C ff.

109. *Iliad* vi.232−36 tells the famous story of the exchange by Glaucus of golden armor for bronze. Socrates is saying that he will not be so easily fooled as to trade real moral beauty for the illusory physical beauty of Alcibiades.

"Still, my dear boy, you should think twice, because you could be wrong, and I may be of no use to you. The mind's sight becomes sharp only when the body's eyes go past their prime—and you are still a good long time away from that."

When I heard this I replied:

"I really have nothing more to say. I've told you exactly what I think. Now it's your turn to consider what you think best for you and me."

"You're right about that," he answered. "In the future, let's   *219B*
consider things together. We'll always do what seems the best to the two of us."

He speaks w/ intent.

His words made me think that my own had finally hit their mark, that he was smitten by my arrows. I didn't give him a chance to say another word. I stood up immediately and placed my mantle over the light cloak which, though it was the middle of winter, was his only clothing. I slipped underneath the cloak and put my arms around this man—this utterly unnatural, this   *219C*
truly extraordinary man—and spent the whole night next to him. Socrates, you can't deny a word of it. But in spite of all my efforts, this hopelessly arrogant, this unbelievably insolent man—he turned me down! He spurned my beauty, of which I was so proud, members of the jury—for this is really what you are: you're here to sit in judgment of Socrates' amazing arrogance and pride. Be sure of it, I swear to you by all the gods and goddesses together, my night with Socrates went no further   *219D*
than if I had spent it with my own father or older brother!

How do you think I felt after that? Of course, I was deeply humiliated, but also I couldn't help admiring his natural character, his moderation, his fortitude—here was a man whose strength and wisdom went beyond my wildest dreams! How could I bring myself to hate him? I couldn't bear to lose his friendship. But how could I possibly win him over? I knew very   *219E*
well that money meant much less to him than enemy weapons ever meant to Ajax,[110] and the only trap by means of which I had thought I might capture him had already proved a dismal failure. I had no idea what to do, no purpose in life; ah, no one else has ever known the real meaning of slavery!

---

110. Ajax, a hero of the Greek army at Troy, carried an enormous shield and so was virtually invulnerable to enemy weapons.

All this had already occurred when Athens invaded Potidaea,[111] where we served together and shared the same mess. Now, first, he took the hardships of the campaign much better than I ever did—much better, in fact, than anyone in the whole army. When we were cut off from our supplies, as often happens

220A in the field, no one else stood up to hunger as well as he did. And yet he was the one man who could really enjoy a feast; and though he didn't much want to drink, when he had to, he could drink the best of us under the table. Still, and most amazingly, no one ever saw him drunk (as we'll straightaway put to the test).

Add to this his amazing resistance to the cold—and, let me
220B tell you, the winter there is something awful. Once, I remember, it was frightfully cold; no one so much as stuck his nose outside. If we absolutely had to leave our tent, we wrapped ourselves in anything we could lay our hands on and tied extra pieces of felt or sheepskin over our boots. Well, Socrates went out in that weather wearing nothing but this same old light cloak, and even in bare feet he made better progress on the ice than the other soldiers did in their boots. You should have seen the looks they
220C gave him; they thought he was only doing it to spite them!

So much for that! But you should hear what else he did during that same campaign,

The exploit our strong-hearted hero dared to do.[112]

One day, at dawn, he started thinking about some problem or other; he just stood outside, trying to figure it out. He couldn't resolve it, but he wouldn't give up. He simply stood there, glued to the same spot. By midday, many soldiers had seen him, and, quite mystified, they told everyone that Socrates had been standing there all day, thinking about something. He was still there when evening came, and after dinner some Ionians moved their
220D bedding outside, where it was cooler and more comfortable (all

---

111. Potidaea, a city in Thrace allied to Athens, was induced by Corinth to revolt in 432 B.C. The city was besieged by the Athenians and eventually defeated in a bloody local war, 432–430 B.C.
112. Homer, *Odyssey* iv.242, 271.

this took place in the summer), but mainly in order to watch if Socrates was going to stay out there all night. And so he did; he stood on the very same spot until dawn! He only left next morning, when the sun came out, and he made his prayers to the new day.

And if you would like to know what he was like in battle— this is a tribute he really deserves. You know that I was decorated for bravery during that campaign: well, during that very battle, Socrates single-handedly saved my life! He absolutely did!   220E
He just refused to leave me behind when I was wounded, and he rescued not only me but my armor as well. For my part, Socrates, I told them right then that the decoration really belonged to you, and you can blame me neither for doing so then nor for saying so now. But the generals, who seemed much more concerned with my social position, insisted on giving the decoration to me, and, I must say, you were more eager than the generals themselves for me to have it.

You should also have seen him at our horrible retreat from Delium.[113] I was there with the cavalry, while Socrates was a foot   221A
soldier. The army had already dispersed in all directions, and Socrates was retreating together with Laches. I happened to see them just by chance, and the moment I did I started shouting encouragements to them, telling them I was never going to leave their side, and so on. That day I had a better opportunity to watch Socrates than I ever had at Potidaea, for, being on horseback, I wasn't in very great danger. Well, it was easy to see that   221B
he was remarkably more collected than Laches. But when I looked again I couldn't get your words, Aristophanes, out of my mind: in the midst of battle he was making his way exactly as he does around town,

   . . . with swagg'ring gait and roving eye.[114]

---

113. At Delium, a town on the Boeotian coastline just north of Attica, a major Athenian expeditionary force was routed by a Boeotian army in 424 B.C. For another description of Socrates' action during the retreat, see *Laches* 181B.

114. Cf. Aristophanes, *Clouds* 362, where the chorus of clouds hails Socrates in similar terms. (. . . σοὶ δὲ / ὅτι βρενθύει τ'ἐν ταῖσιν ὁδοῖς καὶ τώφθαλμὼ παραβάλλεις).

He was observing everything quite calmly, looking out for friendly troops and keeping an eye on the enemy. Even from a great distance it was obvious that this was a very brave man, who would put up a terrific fight if anyone approached him. This is what saved both of them. For, as a rule, you try to put as much distance as you can between yourself and such men in battle; you go after the others, those who run away helter-skelter.

221C

You could say many other marvelous things in praise of Socrates. Perhaps he shares some of his specific accomplishments with others. But, as a whole, he is unique; he is like no one else in the past and no one in the present—this is by far the most amazing thing about him. For we might be able to form an idea of what Achilles was like by comparing him to Brasidas or some other great warrior, or we might compare Pericles with Nestor or Antenor or one of the other great orators.[115] There is a parallel for everyone—everyone else, that is. But this man here is so bizarre, his ways and his ideas are so unusual, that, search as you might, you'll never find anyone else, alive or dead, who's even remotely like him. The best you can do is not to compare him to anything human, but to liken him, as I do, to Silenus and the satyrs, and the same goes for his ideas and arguments.

221D

Come to think of it, I should have mentioned this much earlier: even his ideas and arguments are just like those hollow statues of Silenus. If you were to listen to his arguments, at first they'd strike you as totally ridiculous; they're clothed in words as coarse as the hides worn by the most vulgar satyrs. He's always going on about pack asses, or blacksmiths, or cobblers, or tanners; he's always making the same tired old points in the same tired old words. If you are foolish, or simply unfamiliar with him, you'd find it impossible not to laugh at his arguments. But if

221E

222A

115. Brasidas, among the most effective Spartan generals during the Peloponnesian War, was mortally wounded while defeating the Athenians at Amphipolis in 422 B.C. (Thucydides IV.102–16). Antenor (for the Trojans) and Nestor (for the Greeks) were the legendary wise men of the Trojan War. Pericles was greater than either of these, as he was both a wise man and an effective leader of the Athenians at the height of their power. See above, 215E4, for a tribute to the power of his speech, and see Thucydides II.65 for a tribute to his leadership of Athens.

you see them when they open up like the statues, if you go behind their surface, you'll realize that no other arguments make any sense. They're truly worthy of a god, bursting with figures of virtue inside. They're of great—no, of the greatest—importance for anyone who wants to become a truly good man.

Well, this is my praise of Socrates, though I haven't spared him my reproach, either; I told you how horribly he treated   *222B* me—and not only me but also Charmides, Euthydemus, and many others. He has deceived us all: he presents himself as your lover, and, before you know it, you're in love with him yourself! I warn you, Agathon, don't let him fool you! Remember our torments; be on your guard: don't wait, like the fool in the proverb, to learn your lesson from your own misfortune.[116]   *222C*

He is equating virtue w/ GOODNESS —
Earlier, he defines this goodness as
opposite of his worldly, political pursuits, etc.

---

116. *Iliad* xvii.32.

FINAL
DIALOGUE

ALCIBIADES' FRANKNESS provoked a lot of laughter, especially since it was obvious that he was still in love with Socrates, who immediately said to him:

"You're perfectly sober after all, Alcibiades. Otherwise you could never have concealed your motive so gracefully: how casually you let it drop, almost like an afterthought, at the very end of your speech! As if the real point of all this has not been simply to make trouble between Agathon and me! You think that I should be in love with you and no one else, while you, and no one else, should be in love with Agathon—well, we were *not* deceived; we've seen through your little satyr play. Agathon, my friend, don't let him get away with it: let no one come between us!"

Agathon said to Socrates:

"I'm beginning to think you're right; isn't it proof of that that he literally came between us here on the couch? Why would he do this if he weren't set on separating us? But he won't get away with it; I'm coming right over to lie down next to you."

"Wonderful," Socrates said. "Come here, on my other side."

"My god!" cried Alcibiades. "How I suffer in his hands! He kicks me when I'm down; he never lets me go. Come, don't be selfish, Socrates; at least, let's compromise: let Agathon lie down between us."

"Why, that's impossible," Socrates said. "You have already delivered your praise of me, and now it's my turn to praise whoever's on my right. But if Agathon were next to you, he'd have to praise me all over again instead of having me speak in his honor, as I very much want to do in any case. Don't be jealous; let me praise the boy."

"Oh, marvelous," Agathon cried. "Alcibiades, nothing can make me stay next to you now. I'm moving no matter what. I simply *must* hear what Socrates has to say about me."

"There we go again," said Alcibiades. "It's the same old story:

222D

222E

223A

when Socrates is around, nobody else can even get close to a good-looking man. Look how smoothly and plausibly he found a reason for Agathon to lie down next to him!" 223B

And then, all of a sudden, while Agathon was changing places, a large drunken group, finding the gates open because someone was just leaving, walked into the room and joined the party. There was noise everywhere, and everyone was made to start drinking again in no particular order.

At that point, Aristodemus said, Eryximachus, Phaedrus, and some others among the original guests made their excuses and left. He himself fell asleep and slept for a long time (it was 223C winter, and the nights were quite long). He woke up just as dawn was about to break; the roosters were crowing already. He saw that the others had either left or were asleep on their couches and that only Agathon, Aristophanes, and Socrates were still awake, drinking out of a large cup which they were passing around from left to right. Socrates was talking to them. 223D Aristodemus couldn't remember exactly what they were saying— he'd missed the first part of their discussion, and he was half-asleep anyway—but the main point was that Socrates was trying to prove to them that authors should be able to write both comedy and tragedy: the skillful tragic dramatist should also be a comic poet. He was about to clinch his argument, though, to tell the truth, sleepy as they were, they were hardly able to follow his reasoning. In fact, Aristophanes fell asleep in the middle of the discussion, and very soon thereafter, as day was breaking, Agathon also drifted off.

But after getting them off to sleep, Socrates got up and left, and Aristodemus followed him, as always. He said that Socrates went directly to the Lyceum, washed up, spent the rest of the day just as he always did, and only then, as evening was falling, went home to rest.

SELECTED
BIBLIOGRAPHY

Allen, R. E. "The Elenchus of Agathon: *Symposium* 199c−201c." *The Monist* 50 (1966): 460−463.

Brentlinger, John A. "The Nature of Love," in *The Symposium of Plato*, translated by Suzy Q Groden. Amherst: The University of Massachusetts Press, 1970: 113−129.

Burnet, John. *Platonis Opera*, vol. II. Oxford Classical Texts. Oxford: Clarendon Press, 1903.

Burnyeat, M. F. "Socratic Midwifery, Platonic Inspiration." *Bulletin of the Institute of Classical Studies* 24 (1977): 7−17.

Bury, R. G. *The Symposium of Plato*. Cambridge: Cambridge University Press, 1932.

Cornford, F. M. "The Doctrine of Eros in Plato's *Symposium*." *The Unwritten Philosophy and Other Essays*. Cambridge: Cambridge University Press, 1950: 68−80. Reprinted in Vlastos, *Plato II*: 119−131.

Dover, K. J. "Aristophanes' Speech in Plato's *Symposium*." *Journal of Hellenic Studies* 66 (1966): 41−50.

————. "Eros and Nomos (Plato, *Symposium* 182a−185c)." *Bulletin of the Institute of Classical Studies* 11 (1964): 31−42.

————. *Greek Homosexuality*. New York: Random House, 1978.

————. *Greek Popular Morality in the Time of Plato and Aristotle*. Oxford: Blackwell, 1974.

————. *Plato: Symposium*. Cambridge Greek and Latin Classics. Cambridge: Cambridge University Press, 1980.

————. "The Date of Plato's *Symposium*." *Phronesis* 10 (1965): 1−20.

Edelstein, Ludwig. "The Role of Eryximachus in Plato's *Symposium*." *Ancient Medicine: Selected Papers of Ludwig Edelstein*. Baltimore: The Johns Hopkins University Press, 1971: 153−171.

Gosling, J. C. B. *Plato*. London: Routledge and Kegan Paul, 1973.

Gould, Thomas. *Platonic Love*. London: Routledge and Kegan Paul, 1963.

Guthrie, W. K. C. *A History of Greek Philosophy*, vol. IV. Cambridge: Cambridge University Press, 1975.

Hackforth, R. "Immortality in Plato's *Symposium*." *Classical Review* 64 (1950): 42−45.

Halperin, David M. "Why Is Diotima a Woman?" in his *One Hundred Years of Homosexuality.* New York: Routledge, 1990: 112–151.

Irwin, T. H. *Plato's Moral Theory.* Oxford: Clarendon Press, 1977.

Luce, J. V. "Immortality in Plato's *Symposium.*" *Classical Review* 66 (1952): 137–141.

Markus, R. A. "The Dialectic of Eros in Plato's *Symposium.*" *Downside Review* 73 (1955): 219–230. Reprinted in Vlastos, *Plato II;* 132–143.

Mattingley, H. B. "The Date of Plato's *Symposium.*" *Phronesis* 3 (1958): 31–39.

Moravcsik, J. M. E. "Reason and Eros in the Ascent-Passage of the *Symposium.*" Anton, John P. and Kustas, G. L. *Essays in Ancient Greek Philosophy.* Albany: SUNY Press, 1971: 285–302.

Neumann, H. "Diotima's Concept of Love." *American Journal of Philology* 86 (1965): 33–59.

Nussbaum, Martha C. *The Fragility of Goodness.* Cambridge: Cambridge University Press, 1986.

Nygren, Anders. *Eros and Agape.* English translation by P. S. Watson. New York: Harper and Row, 1969.

Rosen, Stanley. *Plato's Symposium.* New Haven: Yale University Press, 1968.

Santas, Gerasimos. *Plato and Freud: Two Theories of Love.* Oxford: Blackwell, 1988.

Singer, Irving. *The Nature of Love, Plato to Luther.* Chicago: University of Chicago Press, 1984.

Sircello, Guy. *Love and Beauty.* Princeton: Princeton University Press, 1989.

Solmsen, Friedrich. "Parmenides and the Description of Perfect Beauty." *American Journal of Philology* 92 (1971): 62–70.

Vlastos, Gregory. *Plato: A Collection of Critical Essays. Vol. II: Ethics, Politics, Philosophy of Art and Religion.* Garden City: Doubleday, 1971.

———— . "The Individual as Object of Love in Plato." In Vlastos, *Platonic Studies.* 2nd ed. Princeton: Princeton University Press, 1981: 3–42.

ALEXANDER NEHAMAS is Professor of Philosophy, University of Pennsylvania. Along with numerous (and celebrated) articles in the scholarly literature, he is author of *Nietzsche: Life as Literature* (Harvard University Press, 1985).

PAUL WOODRUFF is Chair, Department of Philosophy, University of Texas. His translation, with commentary, of Plato's *Hippias Major* (Hackett, 1982) was selected by *Choice* as an "Outstanding Academic Book" 1982. His radio play *Letter to Rome* was presented on the BBC Third Programme in 1969. *The Prisoners Play*, an opera for children, was presented in Toronto in 1973.

do calc. hw
read eng.
write dl paper